THE
HEALING
SLOW COOKER

THE HEALING SLOW COOKER

Lower Stress
Improve Gut Health
Decrease Inflammation

Jennifer Iserloh

Foreword by Drew Ramsey, MD

Photographs by Alice Gao

CHRONICLE BOOKS
SAN FRANCISCO

Library of Congress Cataloging-in-Publication Data
Names: Iserloh, Jennifer, author. | Gao, Alice, photographer.
Title: The healing slow cooker : lower stress, improve gut health, decrease
inflammation / Jennifer Iserloh ; foreword by Drew Ramsey, M.D.
   ; photographs by Alice Gao.
Description: San Francisco : Chronicle Books, [2017] | Includes
   bibliographical references and index.
Identifiers: LCCN 2017008780 | ISBN 9781452160634 (hc : alk. paper)
Subjects: LCSH: Electric cooking, Slow. | Functional foods. | Health. |
   LCGFT: Cookbooks.
Classification: LCC TX827 .I84 2017 | DDC 641.5/884--dc23 LC record available
at https://lccn.loc.gov/2017008780

ISBN 978-1-4521-6063-4
Manufactured in China
Photographs by Alice Gao
Prop styling by Kira Corbin
Food styling by Chelsea Zimmer
Designed by Vanessa Dina
Typesetting by Frank Brayton

10 9 8 7 6 5 4 3 2 1

Chronicle books and gifts are available at special quantity discounts to
corporations, professional associations, literacy programs, and other organizations.
For details and discount information, please contact our premiums department at
corporatesales@chroniclebooks.com or at 1-800-759-0190.

Chronicle Books LLC
680 Second Street
San Francisco, California 94107
www.chroniclebooks.com

To the power of plants—
may we continue to learn their mysteries
and protect their habitats.

How can we properly nourish ourselves? As a nutritional psychiatrist, I prescribe foods to specifically help people improve their brain health. The best way to get those foods into your body is by cooking meals yourself at home. There are many barriers to preparing food at home (for example, some people don't like to cook or they never learned how), but the one I hear most often is that people are "too busy" to cook.

That's a big challenge at my clinic as we try to help patients increase their intake of nutrient-dense foods: greens, beans, vegetables, seafood, and grass-fed meat. So we offer a list of tools that will help people cook more in the kitchen, and high on that list is a slow cooker. As modern medical science moves toward embracing the ancient wisdom that food is medicine, we've discovered that the slow cooker is one of the easiest ways to create delicious meals that incorporate healthful ingredients.

In fact, "Do you own a slow cooker?" has become one of the screening questions at my clinic in New York City, because I know it makes cooking meals at home easy and doable, particularly for those who are not that savvy in the kitchen. I'm guessing you picked up this book because you have a slow cooker already and you want to know how to use it to cook the most healthful meals possible. Lucky for you, you found this wonderful guide written by Chef Jennifer Iserloh.

Jen is a rare find in the health world. Along with her own books and projects, she is a tireless recipe developer who has enhanced the projects of so many in the health and wellness world. I've worked with her for many years, and Jen's cooking has informed my own—to the betterment of my own health. I remember how she reinvented a traditional tomato-based gazpacho and created an entirely new green version using kiwi, green peppers, and kale—delicious! She has also taught me how certain flavor pairings work together and shared tips and secrets that she's learned from her decades working in the realms of food and health. Jen is particularly skilled with a slow cooker, and thus here she shares her secrets with you.

When you increase nutrient density in your diet, you will get more nourishment in your brain and body with fewer calories. Eating this way not only makes us healthier, it naturally guides our bodies to our optimal weight. Jen shows you how to maximize nutrient density by pairing certain ingredients together for the ultimate synergy—think turmeric and black pepper or cinnamon and legumes. And as you learn about each ingredient, you'll become more savvy about which ones make you less stressed (cardamom) and which ones boost your energy (bone broth).

Taking it slow while you cook makes it easier to slow down in your everyday life. This book is the first step on your path to a healthier you, and the bubbling pot on your counter will fill your kitchen with the heady aroma of health and joy.

To your health,

Drew Ramsey, MD

Healing Foods Can Change Your Life

I've been a health coach and healthy-eating advocate for the past thirteen years, and throughout my career, superfoods and medicinal foods have amazed and inspired me. I first started to understand the impact of food on health when I revamped my eating habits during my time in college. I was in a very different place then—well on my way to becoming obese like many of my family members, and crippled by irritable bowel syndrome. I also had regular bouts of depression and anxiety, all of which kept me from focusing on my studies and enjoying everyday life. At the time, I was a slave to a rampant sugar addiction that was spurred on by consuming plenty of sweets daily. One afternoon, coming home from one of my classes, I was so doubled over with pain that I could barely walk. I felt a deep shame that I was more than thirty pounds overweight. In that moment, I decided to take matters into my own hands.

First, I cut candy bars, sodas, cakes, and pies completely from my diet. I went cold turkey out of fierce determination. In a few weeks, there was a big shift in how I felt, and in a few months, I had lost nearly twenty pounds! I had less stomach pain and I spent less time thinking about sweets, as it became clear that I had been using them as a crutch to soothe emotional upset. I started to clean up my diet by including healthier foods, although I still suffered from bouts of IBS.

In my thirties, I followed my lifelong dream of becoming a chef. I worked professionally in New York City, training in top-rated restaurants. I continued to keep my weight down and eat nourishing meals, despite working in a very tough industry in one of the most competitive cities in the world. But I still had random bouts of IBS and a lot of bloating that I just chalked up to my finicky stomach. I accepted my pain as status quo since a top gastrointestinal specialist who practiced on the Upper East Side of Manhattan said it was all in my head. Since this was long before I knew about eating for gut health, I learned to live with it. Though, even at the time, I was surprised that the doctor never once asked about my diet nor ran any tests.

My understanding of food as medicine took a real turning point after I left the restaurant scene. I started working as a recipe developer on my first book project, *Food Cures*, with Joy Bauer, the nutritionist for the *Today Show*. The book focused on superfoods for condition-specific eating, giving food prescriptions for a wide range of ailments, from migraines to skin conditions to IBS, my personal struggle. Joy taught me so many things, most notably that even healthy whole foods, like fruits and vegetables, can be triggers for chronic illness, depending on the severity of the condition. I also learned that there are superfoods, super-herbs, and superspices that can greatly soothe medical conditions and limit flare-ups. I began to experiment on myself and fine-tuned my diet. I was amazed that many of my IBS issues simply vanished.

I wanted to learn even more about healing foods, so for the past five years, I worked with functional and integrated physicians who taught me how to use a special class of plants called adaptogens (like reishi, goji berries, and turmeric), which you will learn more about and use throughout the book. And through the process (and eating these foods myself), not only did I see the benefits, but I realized that they can easily be incorporated into regular meals for balance and energy.

What Are Superfoods?

Superfoods are called "super" for one reason: they deliver exponentially more nutrition compared with non-superfoods. Foods like kale, spinach, and broccoli outclass other foods in their category since they deliver 50 to 100 percent more of many essential vitamins and minerals per ounce. It's the difference between a cup of kale, which has 75 percent of your recommended daily allowances of vital nutrients vitamins A and C, and the same serving of cucumber, which has only 1 percent vitamin A and 2 percent vitamin C, just to name one example. Once I learned this through my work with Joy, I overhauled my own plate as well as the recipes I created for clients when I was a personal chef.

Adaptogens

Food as medicine goes further than just "an apple a day" or eating your greens, as I learned by working with some of the most progressive doctors in the field. Beyond superfoods, I discovered there was much more to healing foods—even a special class of foods called adaptogens, which up to that point were unknown to me. Adaptogens are very special superfoods: not only do they contain good levels of essential vitamins and minerals, but they also have unique compounds that can modify your biochemistry. They can affect the way your brain functions, how your cells operate, and how smoothly your nervous system runs, and adaptogens are "immune-modulating," which means they help balance your immune system with special compounds that encourage homeostasis, or internal balance.

Unlike superfoods, which are typically nutritive for specific organs, adaptogens have a whole-body balancing effect—you can think of them as more holistic superfoods. Why? They are beneficial for the neuroendocrine system (how your nervous system communicates with your glands) and also help to balance two very important stress hormones: adrenaline and cortisol. This may all seem like a new trend, but adaptogens have actually been used for thousands of years to treat and prevent illness by European and American folk healers, traditional Chinese medicine doctors, and Ayurvedic practitioners. The only new news is that Western medical studies are finally paying attention to adaptogens, proving that these foods have special healing properties.

Synergistic Ingredients

When it comes to getting even more from healing foods—both super-foods and adaptogens—synergy is the name of the game, since when they are paired up they become more nutritious or even more potent. By pairing these foods synergistically (meaning pairing the right foods together, since not all pairings work to boost health effects and some actually block them), there is an interaction that leads to better health in a few ways, such as enabling better absorption of nutrients, keeping nutrients in the body longer, and even making nutrients more potent once inside the gut or brain.

There are many simple and delicious ways you can synergize ingredients that are accomplished for you in the recipes in this book, such as adding good-quality fats to greens rich in fat-soluble vitamins A and D for better absorption (like the recipes you will see containing kale) and pairing vitamin C–rich vegetables with high-iron foods (red bell pepper with spinach or beans) to allow the body to soak in more vitamin C. Spices can also activate each other in astonishing ways, like black pepper and turmeric (you'll see these together in many of the recipes): the compounds in black pepper make curcumin, turmeric's healing compound, 100 per-cent more effective because they keep curcumin in your intestines longer. You'll also see combos like two cancer-fighting foods in one dish, such as onions and garlic, which makes their sulfur compounds three times more potent. But you won't have to study food chemistry to get all of this good stuff. Just pull out your slow cooker and follow the recipes.

Superfoods, Meet the Slow Cooker

The more I learned about superfoods and adaptogens, the more I wanted to cook with them in creative, tasty ways. Now I strive to teach others how to make wonderful healing meals like the ones featured in this book. But two obstacles keep coming up for people who want to cook healthy meals at home: time and know-how.

Using the slow cooker is a simple way to get more healing foods into your body with the least amount of effort. For this book that celebrates the slow-cooking method, I chose to group the recipes that would target common health concerns. In the Detox and Calm chapter, for example, recipes like Green Tea–Shiitake Miso Soup (page 37) and Rooibos Tea–Poached Salmon with Kale (page 45) will help you when you're feeling overwhelmed and stressed. If you need more energy and strength, flip to the Rebuild and Strengthen chapter, where recipes like French Onion Bone Broth Soup (page 60) and Pepper Berry Millet (page 58) will build you up by soothing and strengthening your digestive system. Need to sharpen your brainpower? The recipes featuring chocolate, nuts and seeds, and seafood in the Sharpen and Rewire chapter will give you that added boost. All of my recipes here have been developed to maximize the nutritional value of their healing ingredients. You'll quickly learn how easy it is to turn to your slow cooker for delicious meals that can help bring your body back into balance too.

If you want to get the best from your slow cooker, there are some simple tips and savvy solutions to improve flavor, texture, and appearance. Here are some tips about using specific ingredients and best practices for your slow cooker:

SPICES

Spices work well in slow-cooked meals, but since the slow cooker mutes flavorings in general, I've had to call for almost twice the amount of spices that I do in my stove-top recipes. But, as it turns out, this is great news when it comes to your health, since spices have incredibly high levels of antioxidants and transformative healing compounds. Spices are inexpensive and sugar-free, with only a trace amount of fat and calories. Many of the spices you'll find in this book are already in your spice rack; but if you need to buy new spices, opt for as many whole spices as possible (like black peppercorns, whole nutmegs, and cinnamon sticks) since spices retain their flavor and nutrition best in their whole form. Use a coffee grinder or sharp Microplane to grind or grate your way to a soulfully spiced, slow-cooked meal.

HERBS

Just like with spices, I use a ton of herbs in these slow-cooked meals. Herbs are the friends with benefits of the kitchen—they contribute essential vitamins and minerals, but they also accent the flavors of plain foods so that they taste amazing with hardly any calories and no fat or sugar. No time or interest in chopping fresh herbs? Just toss in the herb sprigs, stems and all—your food will still gain beautiful flavor. Herbs maintain their antioxidant levels even when dried, but I prefer fresh herbs with delicate seafood dishes. For sturdier proteins like chicken and beef, both dried and fresh herbs will do.

SEAFOOD

It may seem unusual to cook seafood in a slow cooker, but this gentle form of moist-heat cooking is ideal for delicate shellfish and fish fillets, which many people tend to overcook on the stove top. If you've never cooked seafood before, you have nothing to fear, because slow-cooked shellfish, salmon, and white fish always come out right. The less fat the seafood contains, the less cooking time it will need, while fattier, oiler fish like salmon take a bit longer—just be sure to follow the time guidelines in the recipes. I always recommend buying skin-on fish to protect it from dryness, but if you don't want the extra work of removing the skin, just ask your fishmonger to do it for you and decrease the cooking time by 15 to 20 minutes.

Seafood is a superfood because it contains body-healing antioxidants, minerals like selenium (for thyroid health), and vitamins B_{12} (for a strong nervous system) and D (for cancer prevention and a healthy brain).

MEAT

Tougher cuts of meat with connective tissues, like beef stew meat, work perfectly in the slow cooker. Using these less expensive cuts is a great way to save cash and also have a tender meat-and-veggie dish for your table. If you want to dabble with grass-fed or more exotic meats, stew meat is the perfect place to start. If previously frozen, the meats will still cook up nicely (just defrost in the fridge overnight), and gamy meats can be heavily flavored with spices. Grass-fed beef is worth the extra cost, since it contains far more health-promoting omega-3s and is leaner and lower in calories than corn-fed beef. Bone-in cuts of other meats, like pork chops and chicken breasts, also lend themselves to slow cooking, since the bones help the leaner meats stay moist as they cook. If it's in your budget, search out pasture-raised pork and organic free-range chicken for the healthiest white meat options.

FATS

Using healthy fats and naturally occurring fats in food (like the fat in salmon) is a great way to prevent foods from drying out while they cook, but generally you can use less fat with moist-heat cooking. The flavor of butter goes an especially long way in a slow cooker: just one tablespoon (to keep calories in check) will nicely flavor the sauce of a whole dish. Opt for grass-fed butter because it's richer in omega-3s (like grass-fed beef). If you don't eat butter but want to add richness to a tomato-based or herb sauce, try coconut oil instead. Olive oil, rich in heart-protective monounsaturated fats, is featured in many of these slow cooker recipes. Sesame oil gives a nutty flavor to Asian dishes and also has some of the same healthy fats you'll find in olive oil. Whichever fat you choose to use, know that you'll also be getting benefits for both your skin and your brain.

LEGUMES, GRAINS, AND ROOT VEGETABLES

Foods like canned beans, steel-cut oats, wild rice, and firmer root vegetables like sweet potatoes and parsnips hold up well in the slow cooker, maintaining their shape as they cook. When cooking with canned beans, be sure to rinse them well under cold running water first for a fresher taste. For dried grains, be sure to pick through them for any debris that you'll want to discard, such as empty husks or the occasional stone. These foods tend to be denser and high in fiber. The fiber helps you to feel full while it feeds the important gut flora that keeps your metabolism from slowing down and safeguards your immunity. So as an added benefit, it also promotes weight loss.

Cooking with Adaptogens

This book is not your standard slow-cooker recipe collection, since it teaches you to use and love a special class of healing foods called adaptogens. They rebalance the immune system, helping you to achieve optimal balance, and give you a leg up when you're facing stress.

What's the key to healthy living on a regular basis? Health experts will agree that it's adapting to stressful circumstances and snapping back after the ups and downs of life. Typically adaptogens are used solo in teas or in supplement form. But in my experience, adaptogens work well in meals too. I've used them to recover after a bout of work exhaustion, or to nip a throat tickle in the bud as I sip my soup. Cooking with adaptogens can be your haven and a yummy rehab to regain balance when you pair them with the superfoods that you'll meet in each chapter.

What's the best place to meet and greet adaptogens? Just open your pantry for starters. Chances are you already have a few of these foods on hand. Black pepper, ginger, and turmeric all fall into this category, and the others in the following section can be easily sourced online, in health-food stores, or even on the shelves at your local grocery store. The key to cooking with adaptogens is knowing when to use them to unlock their active compounds and maximize their healing potential. The recipes here are engineered to get the most out of these ingredients and make them taste good, all while unlocking more healing benefits.

BLACK PEPPER

Piperine, the active ingredient in black pepper, helps to increase nutrient absorption. It's also touted for memory and liver protection and as an anti-inflammatory and tumor-suppressing compound. Preground pepper can lose its flavor over time, and when it is exposed to extended heat and light, its active compounds like piperine and other antioxidants can be damaged. I suggest freshly grinding or cracking whole black peppercorns just before use.

GOJI BERRY (CHINESE WOLFBERRY)

The group of active ingredients that give goji berries their get-up-and-go are called arabinogalactans. These compounds help your cells signal more efficiently to trigger your immunity response to cope with disease. The goji berry helps protect the liver, improve kidney function, enhance your immune system, and boost the microbiome (gut bacteria). Extensive testing has shown that the goji berry is completely nontoxic and is a great adaptogen that combines powerfully with superfoods like nuts and seeds and other adaptogens such as turmeric. Dried goji berries are easy to eat and retain their nutrition, but if you have a sensitive stomach, you can make them easier to digest. Just crush them in a mortar and pestle or blender and soak in a few tablespoons of warm water for eight to ten minutes.

GINGER

Gingerols, a very healing group of active compounds in ginger, have been studied for their ability to soothe pain by turning off pain receptors. Gingerols are protective for many systems and organs in the body because they are very high in anti-inflammatory compounds and other compounds that actually stop spasms. Gingerols have been shown to benefit nerve cells, gastrointestinal health, joints, and the liver and kidneys. For the best quality, shop for fresh ginger that has a tight, smooth beige skin with no blemishes. Once peeled, the root inside should be bright yellow; if it's green or has a black strip, it's beginning to spoil.

MUSHROOMS

Terpenoids are the active ingredients in mushrooms that are heart-protective, since they reduce inflammation as well as working as an antifungal, antibacterial, antiviral, and antitumor compound. To get the most out of mushrooms and their healing compounds, be sure their caps aren't damaged in any way. Buy mushrooms that have firm caps that are free of cracks, black or slimy spots, spoilage, or mold, all of which can damage the healing compounds.

Synergistic Food Pairings

As you've learned, pairing certain ingredients can make them more potent, easier for your body to absorb, and in some cases even tastier and more visually appealing. Learn from the simple pairings that follow to see how to combine spices, herbs, adaptogenic foods, and superfoods for the healthiest combinations around. Once you understand which foods enhance other foods, you can experiment with other dishes or even just simple snacks to reap the benefits of these enhanced pairings.

ALMONDS WITH SEEDS AND GRAINS

Almonds paired with grains and seeds, like you'll find in Chocolate-Almond Quinoa Breakfast with Raspberries (page 103), is a double plus for the circulatory system and the heart. Together, they contain all the most important heart-healthy nutrients. Vitamin E, the heart-detoxifying fat, and potassium, a mineral that calms blood pressure, are found in almonds, while millet and quinoa provide a hefty dose of the magnesium and manganese that are essential for proper blood flow and calm blood vessels.

BLACK PEPPER WITH TURMERIC

Black pepper isn't just a run-of-the-mill spice, it's a superfood for the brain and also works as a turbocharger for turmeric. Black pepper perks up turmeric's astringent flavor while magnifying its active compounds, and black pepper also increases turmeric's absorption by 100 percent. Add freshly ground black pepper whenever you use turmeric—the preground spice loses flavor and potency. You'll find this combo in many recipes ahead, such as Slow Cooker Golden Yogurt (page 57) and Chili-Chocolate Black Beans with Chorizo (page 109).

CINNAMON WITH BEANS

Sweet cinnamon pairs beautifully with bland yet creamy beans, like in my recipe for Shredded Cinnamon Beef Chili with Black Beans (page 97). You'll find it is already used this way in many food traditions from around the word, such as Indian, Mexican, and Middle Eastern fare. Cinnamon is touted for its ability to steady blood sugar and that's due to its high levels of manganese. Pairing cinnamon with a high-fiber, high-antioxidant food like beans is a one-two punch for diabetes prevention. Cinnamon works well with any sweet preparation, including cooked fruit, breakfast cereal, and dessert. Cinnamon tastes delicious with dairy, and the fats in dairy magnify the flavor of cinnamon.

KALE AND OTHER CRUCIFERS AND HEALTHY FATS

Using healthy fats like olive oil, coconut oil, and sesame oil, as well as grass-fed butter, is always a smart idea; these can be found in my Green Tea–Shiitake Miso Soup (page 37) and Shrimp Scampi with Wilted Kale (page 48). Not only do healthy fats enhance the flavor of slightly bitter cruciferous veggies like broccoli and cauliflower, they also boost uptake of the vitamin A found in these veggies. Cruciferous vegetables pair well with pasture-raised pork products, grass-fed beef, and hard and soft cheeses. Kale is more nutritious cooked, which activates fibers that help with cholesterol control and gut health and is safer for those with thyroid issues.

GARLIC WITH ONIONS

The pairing of garlic with onions tastes great, and both are low in calories but big on flavor from their potent sulfur-based compounds (the ones that bring tears to your eyes when you slice onions and leave that unmistakable aroma on your fingers when you mince garlic cloves). For slow cooker recipes, any traditional recipe that calls for either garlic or onions would certainly benefit from the addition of the other, such as in my Mushroom and Garlic Scape Risotto (page 42) and Shredded Flank Steak au Poivre (page 69). To play around with pairing these ingredients, simply add two garlic cloves per one chopped onion in any recipe. The wide variety of detoxing compounds when garlic and onion are combined boosts the health of many systems in the body, such as the liver, and heart and blood circulation.

CHAPTER 1

DETOX AND CALM

MEET THE INGREDIENTS:
Kale, Cardamom, Mushrooms, Oregano, Tea

DETOX AND CALM

Cleanse, Soothe and Clear Inflammation, Calm

Feeling stressed? Don't blame it all on your job. What you are eating could have more to do with it than you think. Constant low-grade inflammation can be caused by many factors, but diet also plays a huge role. Though most people understand the importance of proper healing from injuries that cause temporary inflammation, fewer realize that chronic low-level amounts of inflammation can have harmful long-term effects.

So which is the bigger issue when it comes to inflammation: stress or food? Think of stress and poor diet as a "chicken and egg" issue—they can both play equal parts and even feed off each other. High levels of stress set you up for making bad food choices because stress makes your hormones go haywire, while poor food choices can damage you on a chemical level, from the gut bacteria in your large intestine to your cells. Combine that with a high-stress job and limited time for preparing healthy foods, and it's not surprising that you'd pick up a doughnut instead of eating a fresh kale salad. Poor eating habits, in turn, trigger low metabolic function and compromised immunity. Eating poorly not only causes general inflammation in the body, but also causes increased cortisol release, which can pitch you into low moods and bring even more stress. And so starts a vicious cycle of reaching out for more of the same poor-quality foods.

The key to breaking the chain—by lowering stress and achieving a sense of calm—is to eat loads of antioxidant-rich, nutrient-dense foods, such as kale, mushrooms, spinach, beans, spices, and herbs. And this can be done so easily when you use your slow cooker.

When it comes to choosing ingredients that cleanse, soothe, clear, and calm, what you leave out of your diet is just as important as what you put in. Foods like refined sugar, white flour, gluten, and corn-fed meat and dairy products can send your body into an inflamed tailspin. You should also stay away from foods that contain trans fats, artificial colorings, and preservatives. You can naturally avoid these trigger foods by making the recipes you'll find in this chapter. The recipes here replace those inflammatory ingredients with superprotective foods like kale, cardamom, mushrooms, oregano, and tea. These heavy hitters both quench inflammation and speed up cleansing processes on a cellular level. They also work hand in hand with internal organs like your intestines and liver, which do the heavy lifting to remove toxins from your body.

Kale, Cardamom, Mushrooms, Oregano, Tea

Kale
Cleanse

Kale is king when it comes to cleansing, since it contains three power-house detoxers that target your liver, cells, and heart. First, it delivers high levels of sulforaphane, a molecule that naturally increases your liver's enzymes, which helps it process toxins faster. Second is kaemp-ferol, which boosts health in the mitochondria—the part of the cell that turns glucose into energy and also activates the longevity gene. Quer-cetin is the third potent antioxidant in play. It calms inflammation with its cancer-fighting ability while also helping to prevent the formation of plaque in blood vessels.

Cardamom
Soothe

Stress can hit hard throughout the body, but it will most likely manifest in your gut first. Cardamom, a little-used spice in America, has a pleas-ant peppery, minty flavor and a powerful soothing effect on digestion. It contains compounds that are antibacterial and antispasmodic, both a boon when your digestion is out of whack from daily stress. Apart from your skin, your liver is the biggest detox organ. When your liver is clogged, your whole body can feel lethargic. Adding cardamom to your diet, along with plenty of greens and other liver-healing foods, will help the liver process toxins more efficiently.

Mushrooms
Clear

Mushrooms have long been prized in folk medicine as a catch-all for healing. Like the other ingredients in this chapter, mushrooms are superhealers for the liver, but they also have a multitude of other health-promoting properties: they are antiatherogenic (preventing fatty deposits in the arteries), antimicrobial, antitumor, and antiviral, just to name a few. Some exotic mushroom varieties, such as reishi and turkey tail, are prized for their exceptional medicinal properties. However, studies show that even the humble button mushroom contains high levels of active healing compounds, such as antiviral *Ganodermas*. Other medicinal mushrooms, like the Russian chaga, have been found to kill cancer cells selectively and stimulate the immune system.

Oregano
Clear

I first used oregano as a medicinal food when I used oregano oil to clear up a nagging sore throat. It took just two doses and less than two days. The antibacterial properties of oregano are well known, and it's the herb that ranks highest on the ORAC scale (the scale that ranks antioxidant load for foods) due to its strong levels of antioxidants. In fact, two of the active compounds in oregano oil, thymol and carvacrol, have even been shown to inhibit growth of bacteria like staphylococcus, which can cause serious infection and illness.

Tea
Calm

Most people think of tea as a drink, but I see its potential as a broth and as a flavoring to enhance food. All teas—including green, black, and herbal—contain inflammation-calming molecules, although green tea seems to have the highest amount of research behind it. Studies say that it works like an inflammation inhibitor because it increases production of interleukin 10, an anti-inflammatory cytokine, or protein, that regulates how cells grow and age.

HIBISCUS-RASPBERRY POACHED PEARS

Bright red, slightly sweet hibiscus tea comes from the tuba-shaped flowers of the hibiscus plant, which get their red color from a potent compound called anthocyanin. Pairing hibiscus tea with juicy, fiber-rich pears can help steady blood sugar, and the very high antioxidant levels in hibiscus blooms have been shown to calm blood pressure. Use this delicious juicy dish as a sweet breakfast or a healthy way to quell a sweet tooth in the afternoon. For spice lovers, add an extra sprinkle of cinnamon on top.

SERVES 8

4 pears

2 cups [240 g] frozen or fresh raspberries or cranberries

1 tsp vanilla extract

½ tsp ground cardamom or 6 green cardamom pods

½ tsp ground cinnamon

½ tsp stevia

2 hibiscus tea bags

2 cups [480 g] plain Greek yogurt

Cut each pear in half lengthwise, leaving the stems intact. Scoop out the cores with a melon baller or cut them out with a paring knife. Place the pears skin-side down in the slow cooker. Add the raspberries, 2 cups [480 ml] water, vanilla, cardamom, cinnamon, and stevia. Remove the tags from the tea bags and tuck the tea bags among the pears. Cover the slow cooker and cook on the high setting for 3 hours, until the pears are tender and the berries form a sauce. Discard the tea bags.

Using a large spoon, place each pear half on a plate and top with a few tablespoons of the berry sauce and ¼ cup of the yogurt. Serve immediately.

Nutritional Stats per Serving
150 calories, 5 g protein, 21 g carbohydrates, 6 g fat (5 g saturated fat), 10 mg cholesterol, 13 g sugars, 5 g fiber, 33 mg sodium

COCONUT-CARDAMOM
RICE PUDDING

Creamy, rich rice pudding may not seem like a cleansing meal, but this *Healing Slow Cooker* version encourages detox because it uses coconut milk instead of potential allergens like eggs and dairy. Adding cardamom not only adds a layer of spice, but also soothes digestion while delivering cancer-fighting compounds. Short-grain brown rice lends itself to slow cooking and is far superior in both texture and taste compared with long-grain or basmati brown rice. Enjoy this in place of your morning cereal or pack it for an on-the-go snack or low-sugar dessert.

SERVES 10

1 cup [200 g] short-grain brown rice

One 14-oz [420-ml] can full-fat coconut milk

2 tsp stevia

2 tsp vanilla extract

1 tsp ground cinnamon

1 tsp ground cardamom

¼ tsp freshly grated nutmeg

Put the rice, coconut milk, stevia, vanilla, cinnamon, cardamom, and nutmeg in the slow cooker. Add 4 cups [960 ml] water and stir to combine. Cover the slow cooker and cook on the low setting for 3 to 3½ hours, until the rice is tender and the liquid is absorbed. Add an additional ½ to 1 cup [120 to 240 ml] water during the last 30 minutes of cooking if the mixture becomes too dry. Serve immediately or cool completely and store in an airtight container in the refrigerator for up to 1 week.

Nutritional Stats per Serving
147 calories, 2 g protein, 16 g carbohydrates, 10 g fat (8 g saturated fat), 0 mg cholesterol, 0 g sugars, 1 g fiber, 6 mg sodium

GREEN TEA–SHIITAKE MISO SOUP

Tea isn't just for teetotalers, it's for those looking for extra flavor, more nutrients, and a simple antioxidant boost to their everyday meals. Studies show that the catechins in green tea make it a great detox partner because it helps boost the breakdown of fat (toxins linger longest in fat cells). The slow cooker uses gentle, moist heat, which is the ideal way to extract the tea's healing compounds and infuse its flavor into the dish. Chinese black vinegar is easy to find in Asian grocery stores and has a deep flavor that's reminiscent of balsamic.

SERVES 6

8 cups [2 L] chicken broth, Basic Bone Broth (page 59), or vegetable broth

¼ cup [60 ml] Chinese black vinegar or balsamic vinegar

3 Tbsp white miso paste

4 green tea bags

1 lb [455 g] shiitake mushrooms, stemmed and sliced

2 cups [30 g] chopped kale

6 scallions, thinly sliced, green and white parts

4 garlic cloves, minced

2 Tbsp Asian sesame oil

6 Tbsp chopped fresh cilantro

Put the broth, vinegar, and miso paste in the slow cooker and whisk well to combine. Remove the tags from the tea bags and tuck the tea bags into the broth mixture. Add the mushrooms, kale, scallions, and garlic, and toss with tongs until the vegetables are coated in the broth mixture. Cover the slow cooker and cook on the low setting for 2 to 2½ hours, until the mushrooms and kale are tender. Discard the tea bags.

Spoon into bowls. Drizzle each serving with 1 teaspoon sesame oil and sprinkle each with 1 tablespoon cilantro. Serve immediately.

CHEF'S NOTE: To turn this soup into a more filling meal, add 1 lb [455 g] peeled, deveined shrimp or 1 lb [455 g] cubed chicken breast meat to the slow cooker along with the vegetables.

Nutritional Stats per Serving
220 calories, 2 g protein, 20 g carbohydrates, 14 g fat (1 g saturated fat), 0 mg cholesterol, 11 g sugars, 2 g fiber, 527 mg sodium

COCONUT CREAM
OF MUSHROOM SOUP

Mushrooms are a treasure chest of healing due to the bioactive compounds they possess called *Ganodermas*. Studies suggest that these compounds offer heart-soothing, tumor-fighting, and brain-boosting benefits. But mushrooms alone do not a meal make, so combining them with a protein-filled broth, healthy fats like coconut oil, and the earthy flavors of oregano—a natural antibacterial—turns the simple mushroom into a healing, savory soup. One of the easiest ways to try out medicinal mushrooms, like the reishi or chaga in this recipe, is to enjoy them in teas that you can find in your local health-food store or online.

SERVES 4

2 lb [910 g] shiitake mushrooms, stemmed and sliced, or portobello mushrooms, stemmed, gills removed, and sliced

1 sweet onion, such as Vidalia, chopped

1 Tbsp coconut or olive oil

1 tsp dried oregano

½ tsp garlic salt

4 cups [960 ml] Basic Bone Broth (page 59) or chicken broth

One 14-oz [420-ml] can full-fat coconut milk

1 reishi or chaga tea bag (optional)

Place the mushrooms, onion, oil, oregano, and garlic salt in the slow cooker and toss well. Cover the slow cooker and cook on the low setting for 1 to 1½ hours, until the mushrooms become tender.

Add the broth and coconut milk to the slow cooker and stir well. Remove the tag from the tea bag (if using) and tuck the tea bag into the mushroom mixture. Cover the slow cooker and cook on the low setting for another 1 to 1½ hours, to allow the tea to steep. Discard the tea bag.

Using an immersion blender, purée until smooth. Spoon into bowls and serve immediately.

Nutritional Stats per Serving

333 calories, 14 g protein, 19 g carbohydrates, 18 g fat (16 g saturated fat), 0 mg cholesterol, 6 g sugars, 5 g fiber, 205 mg sodium

CARDAMOM-ORANGE QUINOA WITH CARROTS

Both grains and seeds contain two detoxing nutrients—manganese, which helps control blood sugar, and magnesium, which helps boost your ability to ward off inflammation. Quinoa is a great, neutral base for layering a variety of flavors, and the combination of orange and cardamom is particularly good. Cardamom, a minty spice with a hint of pepper flavor, also adds cancer-preventive compounds that are being studied for their ability to ward off skin cancer.

SERVES 8

2 oranges

1 cup [180 g] red, white, or black quinoa, rinsed well under cold water

2½ cups [600 ml] chicken broth, vegetable broth, or Basic Bone Broth (page 59)

1 lb [455 g] carrots, peeled and sliced

⅓ cup [45 g] golden raisins

One 1-in [2.5-cm] piece fresh ginger, peeled and minced

1 tsp ground cardamom

½ tsp salt

½ tsp freshly ground black pepper

Zest the oranges, and reserve the fruit.

Put the quinoa, broth, carrots, raisins, ginger, cardamom, salt, black pepper, and orange zest in a slow cooker and stir well. Cover the slow cooker and cook on the low setting for 3 to 3½ hours, until the quinoa is tender.

Using a chef's knife, cut the peel from the oranges. To segment the oranges, work over a large bowl. Holding the peeled orange in your hand, use a small paring knife to slice between the white membranes of the orange to free the segments and allow them to drop into the bowl as you continue on to the next segment. Repeat with the remaining orange.

CONT'D

Spoon the quinoa into bowls and top each serving with a few orange segments. Serve immediately.

Nutritional Stats per Serving
170 calories, 5 g protein, 31 g carbohydrates, 3 g fat (1 g saturated fat), 1 mg cholesterol, 11 g sugars, 5 g fiber, 230 mg sodium

MUSHROOM AND GARLIC SCAPE RISOTTO

Garlic scapes are the flower stalks of the garlic plant, which can be hard to find, so seek them out at farmers' markets or fine grocery stores in summertime. They can be used like scallions, though they have a slightly tougher texture. Their flavors go well with the shiitake mushrooms called for here. If you can find chaga mushroom tea bags, I suggest you try them. Some studies show that the chaga mushroom can stimulate the immune system and possibly fight certain cancer cells. Making risotto in a slow cooker is a snap. There's no need for continuous stirring—just mix everything together, hit the start button, and tick off things on your to-do list while it cooks. Short-grain brown rice is a must since its naturally chewy, dense texture doesn't become soggy during slow cooking.

SERVES 6

2 cups [200 g] short-grain brown rice

4 cups [960 ml] chicken broth or mushroom broth

1 sweet onion, such as Vidalia, chopped

4 garlic cloves, minced

1 lb [455 g] shiitake mushrooms, stemmed and sliced

½ tsp garlic salt

¼ tsp freshly ground black pepper

2 reishi or chaga tea bags (optional)

¼ cup [60 g] mascarpone cheese or coconut cream

½ cup [15 g] grated Parmesan

2 Tbsp grass-fed butter

2 cups [80 g] microgreens or chopped fresh basil stems and leaves

4 thinly sliced garlic scapes or scallions, green and white parts

Put the rice, broth, onion, garlic, mushrooms, garlic salt, and pepper in the slow cooker and mix together. Remove the tags from the tea bags (if using) and tuck the tea bags into the rice mixture. Cover the slow cooker and cook on the low setting for 1½ to 2 hours, until the rice is tender and most of the liquid is absorbed. Discard the tea bags.

Add the mascarpone, Parmesan, and butter and stir until incorporated.

Spoon into bowls and garnish with the microgreens and garlic scapes. Serve immediately.

Nutritional Stats per Serving

407 calories, 13 g protein, 57 g carbohydrates, 17 g fat (8 g saturated fat), 43 mg cholesterol, 4 g sugars, 6 g fiber, 296 mg sodium

BUTTERNUT SHEPHERD'S PIES

Shepherd's pie is a British meat casserole that traditionally uses leftover stew as its base and has a fluffy mashed potato topping. It works beautifully when you use your slow cooker as the casserole dish and layer the ingredients. This vegetarian take on what is normally a meat-and-potato comfort meal relies on umami-rich mushrooms in place of meat. Umami is one of the five basic tastes and is responsible for rich, savory flavors that can be similar to meat. Mushrooms contain nerve-regenerating properties that will keep you calm long after you nosh. Butternut squash is a great high-nutrient alternative to the traditional mashed potatoes in this recipe, and it delivers extra-high levels of vitamin A, a top nutrient for protecting skin from cold and wind damage.

SERVES 8

2 lb [910 g] portobello mushrooms, stemmed, gills removed, and sliced

1 onion, minced

4 garlic cloves, minced

2 Tbsp coconut or olive oil

2 Tbsp tomato paste

½ tsp salt

¼ tsp freshly ground black pepper

Two 15-oz [425-g] cans butternut squash purée

½ cup [120 ml] heavy cream or canned full-fat coconut milk

2 Tbsp grated fresh ginger

2 tsp baking soda

Put the mushrooms, onion, garlic, oil, tomato paste, ¼ teaspoon salt, and the pepper in the slow cooker and toss well to combine.

In a large bowl, whisk together the butternut squash purée, heavy cream, ginger, baking soda, and remaining ¼ teaspoon salt. Spoon the squash mixture evenly over the mushroom mixture. Cover the slow cooker and cook on the low setting for 2 to 2½ hours, until the mushrooms are tender and the butternut squash mixture is hot.

Use a large spatula or serving spoon to transfer to bowls. Serve immediately.

Nutritional Stats per Serving
248 calories, 5 g protein, 33 g carbohydrates, 12 g fat (7 g saturated fat), 27 mg cholesterol, 7 g sugars, 5 g fiber, 593 mg sodium

ROOIBOS TEA–POACHED SALMON WITH KALE

Rooibos tea (also called red bush) is a rich, slightly sweet, caramel-flavored red tea that is made from drying the leaves of a South Africa bush. It's high in antioxidants and soothing compounds and has the added advantage of being naturally caffeine-free. Kale is rich in a wide array of nutrients, making it an excellent detox partner. It's especially high in C, a vitamin that doesn't get damaged during the slow-cooking process. Be sure to drink the broth, as water-soluble vitamins and other nutrients are captured in the liquid. To make this meal heartier, add a gluten-free corn muffin or other gluten-free bread to soak up the delicious juices.

SERVES 4

Four 4-oz [115-g] skin-on salmon fillets

1 Tbsp coconut or olive oil

4 garlic cloves, minced

½ tsp salt

½ tsp freshly ground black pepper

4 rooibos tea bags

1 lb [455 g] baby kale or baby spinach

Place the salmon skin-side down in the slow cooker. Drizzle with the oil and sprinkle with the garlic, salt, and pepper. Add enough water to just cover the salmon. Remove the tags from the tea bags and tuck the tea bags among the fillets. Cover the slow cooker and cook on the low setting for 1 to 1½ hours, until the salmon is cooked and the fish flakes when pressed with a fork.

Transfer the salmon to a plate and cover with aluminum foil, leaving any cooking juices behind to cook the kale. Discard the tea bags.

Put the kale in the slow cooker (no need to wash the slow cooker). Cover the slow cooker and cook on the high setting for 20 minutes, until the kale wilts.

Transfer the kale and the cooking juices to wide shallow bowls and top with the salmon. Serve immediately.

Nutritional Stats per Serving
203 calories, 24 g protein, 6 g carbohydrates, 9 g fat (4 g saturated fat), 45 mg cholesterol, 9 g sugars, 1 g fiber, 400 mg sodium

MARCONA ALMOND TROUT OVER KALE SUCCOTASH

Kale, the king of cruciferous vegetables, makes a nutritious base for this flaky fish dish. Kale not only helps the liver process toxins faster and calms inflammation, it's also more nutritious when it's cooked versus served raw. Top the dish off with fat-rich Marcona almonds, which have a broader, rounder shape and a more delicate, sweeter taste than regular almonds. Plus, they aid in nutrient uptake and add a pleasing crunch to the dish. If you can't find Marcona almonds, toasted whole almonds, with skins intact, will do just as well.

SERVES 6

2 lemons

½ cup [50 g] chopped Marcona almonds

½ cup [70 g] pitted black olives

¼ cup [10 g] chopped fresh flat-leaf parsley

2 Tbsp coconut or olive oil

½ tsp salt

¼ tsp freshly ground black pepper

One 12-oz [340-g] package frozen succotash, defrosted

4 cups [60 g] chopped kale, such as curly or lacinato

Six 4-oz [115-g] skin-on trout fillets

Zest the lemons, then cut the zested lemons into quarters, reserving them for serving. In a small bowl, stir together the lemon zest, almonds, olives, parsley, 1 Tbsp of the oil, the salt, and the pepper.

Put the succotash, kale, and the remaining 1 Tbsp oil in the slow cooker and toss well. Spread the succotash mixture in an even layer. Place the trout skin-side down on top of the succotash mixture and sprinkle with the almond mixture. Cover the slow cooker and cook on the low setting for 1 to 1½ hours, until the trout flakes when pressed with a fork.

Transfer the trout to plates and spoon the succotash mixture next to the trout. Serve immediately with the lemon wedges on the side.

Nutritional Stats per Serving

279 calories, 21 g protein, 17 g carbohydrates, 15 g fat (4 g saturated fat), 47 mg cholesterol, 1 g sugars, 4 g fiber, 458 mg sodium

SHRIMP SCAMPI WITH WILTED KALE

This is an easy appetizer you can whip together while the wine is chilling; I recommend a sparkling rosé or a dry white wine with citrus notes, like Sauvignon Blanc. Garlic and kale not only taste amazing together, they both contain major detox components that give your liver a boost and are cancer-protective. To make this a heartier meal, serve it over the Cardamom-Orange Quinoa with Carrots (page 39) or cooked grains of your choice.

SERVES 8

4 Tbsp [55 g] grass-fed butter, at room temperature

8 garlic cloves, minced

¼ tsp salt

½ tsp freshly ground black pepper

2 lb [910 g] peeled, deveined medium shrimp

10 oz [280 g] baby kale or baby spinach

Put the butter, garlic, salt, and black pepper in the slow cooker and stir well. Place the shrimp on top of the butter mixture. Cover the slow cooker and cook on the low setting for 1 to 1½ hours, until the shrimp are nearly cooked through.

Scatter the kale over the shrimp, cover the slow cooker, and cook on the low setting for 30 minutes more, until the kale wilts. Spoon the shrimp and kale onto plates. Serve immediately.

Nutritional Stats per Serving
193 calories, 24 g protein, 6 g carbohydrates, 7 g fat (4 g saturated fat), 256 mg cholesterol, 1 g sugars, 1 g fiber, 256 mg sodium

CHICKEN BASIL KALE VERDE

Refreshing tomatillos, also called Mexican husk tomatoes, give a tangy, almost citrus flavor to this easy sauce. Including herbs isn't just for flavor: common culinary basil can help boost better circulation, since it contains vitamin K and eugenol, a heart-protecting, cancer-fighting compound. Pairing basil with kale is also heart smart. Kale contains extremely high levels of carotenoids, which turn to vitamin A in the body, a preventative vitamin for your heart as well as many other organs.

SERVES 4

4 tomatillos, husked

2 cups [30 g] chopped baby kale

1 cup [12 g] packed fresh basil leaves

½ onion, minced

½ tsp salt

Two 15-oz [425-g] cans chickpeas, drained and rinsed

Four 6-oz [170-g] boneless, skinless chicken breasts

½ cup [120 ml] sour cream (optional)

Rinse the tomatillos well and put them in the slow cooker. Add 2 Tbsp water, cover the slow cooker, and cook on the high setting for 1 hour, until the tomatillos are soft. Transfer the tomatillos to a plate to cool for 5 minutes.

While the tomatillos cool, put the kale, basil, onion, and salt in a food processor and process until finely chopped. Add the cooled tomatillos (no need to chop them) and pulse until a salsa forms.

Put the chickpeas in the slow cooker (no need to wash the slow cooker). Place the chicken breasts on top of the chickpeas and drizzle with half of the salsa. Cover the slow cooker and cook on the low setting for 1½ to 2 hours, until the chicken is cooked through and no longer pink in the center.

CONT'D

Transfer the chicken to plates and spoon the sauce along with the chickpea-basil mixture over the top. Serve immediately with sour cream (if using) and remaining salsa.

———————————————————————————

Nutritional Stats per Serving (without sour cream)
475 calories, 66 g protein, 26 g carbohydrates, 14 g fat (5 g saturated fat), 167 mg cholesterol, 4 g sugars, 6 g fiber, 740 mg sodium

CHAPTER 2

REBUILD AND STRENGTHEN

MEET THE INGREDIENTS:
Black Pepper, Probiotic and
Prebiotic Foods, Bone Broth, Berries

REBUILD AND STRENGTHEN

Boost Gut Health, Strengthen Digestion

Does your gut instinct tell you that something's off? Maybe it's your gut! If you would like to rebuild the strength of your digestion and immunity from the inside out, start with foods that are kind to your digestive tract. Your microbiome (that jungle of microorganisms that live in your gut) is responsible for not only proper digestion but also your energy levels, immunity, mood, and how efficiently you utilize and burn calories.

Doctors and current medical research point to poor gut health as the culprit behind autoimmune diseases, gastrointestinal issues, allergies, and chronic fatigue. The foods you eat play a huge role in boosting or depleting your microbiome. Foods to avoid include inflammatory foods like trans fats and hydrogenated fats, processed white sugar, gluten, and artificial colorings and preservatives.

You don't need to go through strict cleanses or fancy diets to maintain gut health (unless you've had serious gastrointestinal issues, in which case you should talk to your doctor). Start by adding simple ingredients like black pepper, bone broth, berries, and foods rich in prebiotics (special fibrous foods that feed gut flora) and probiotics (fermented foods that contain the same flora that's in your gut) to seal and reseed your gut. Look for meat and dairy products with labels that say they come from grass-fed animals and avoid dairy with added hormones and other artificial additives you don't want or need. Avoid gluten, a protein found in wheat, barley, and rye, since it's a major disruptor for anyone with gastrointestinal problems, immunity issues, thyroid struggles, or any autoimmune illness.

Black Pepper, Probiotic and Prebiotic Foods, Bone Broth, Berries

Black Pepper
Boost and Strengthen

Simple, everyday black pepper carries a hidden powerhouse compound called piperine; this megabooster (or bioenhancer) improves nutrient uptake as it travels from your digestive tract into your blood and brain. Piperine also keeps nutrients in your body longer so they have a better likelihood of being absorbed.

Black pepper is unique because it not only contains compounds that protect the liver but also increases the bioavailability of antioxidants— how well you take them in from food versus just having the compounds pass through your digestive tract and straight out of the body, unused.

Black pepper has been used in folk and Ayurvedic medicine as a warming spice to improve digestion, because the minute you eat it, your salivary glands activate enzymes like amylase that increase the rate at which you digest food. Black pepper also raises your body temperature (much like spicy chiles), which helps you burn calories faster and gives you a subtle warming sensation that can add a layer of comfort to your dishes.

But black pepper's benefits are even hotter on a biological level. In current medical research, piperine is prized for its ability to work on a cellular level as a cancer-inhibitor, tumor-suppressor, and anti-inflammatory.

Probiotic and Prebiotic Foods
Boost and Strengthen

Feeding your gut properly is more than just filling up with regular foods that everyone knows are healthy, like veggies, fruits, nuts, and seeds. In this chapter, you'll learn to nourish your gut bugs with nosh that's beneficial for them, including bone broths, probiotic foods, and spices. Probiotic foods, which contain friendly gut bacteria—the same ones that live in your gut—are found in foods like cultured dairy. These foods can help reseed your gut when it's in need. Prebiotic foods like carrots, onions, garlic, and asparagus provide oligosaccharides, a type of natural vegetable sugar upon which gut bacteria feast, making them strong and hearty to ward off enemy bacteria and fungal growth that can come from stress, eating spoiled foods, and consuming too much sugar.

Bone Broth

Strengthen

The popularity of bone broth is on the rise since it has an old-fashioned soulful taste. Research shows that its benefits are more limited than most health nuts claim—it's not as high in mineral content as some believe—but GI docs will agree that it's good for gut repair. It's high in gelatin that can help heal perforations in the gut lining, making it the perfect restorative when you've overdone it the night before on alcohol, sugar, gluten, and other "treats" that can cause the delicate tissues of the small intestine to tear.

Berries

Strengthen

Sweet, delightful blueberries, raspberries, strawberries, and goji berries feed your craving for sweets while also supporting your microbiome. They are a boon for the gut microbiota since, like prebiotic food, they feed the microbes with pectin and the natural sugars occurring in the berries, called polysaccharides. They can also keep hunger pangs at bay by filling you up with plenty of fiber that helps to stabilize your blood sugar and make you feel full with fewer calories. A diet that's rich in berries can also help with regular elimination, the ultimate detox function of the body. Plus, they are a treat that you can enjoy without guilt.

SLOW COOKER GOLDEN YOGURT

Yogurt is a delicious easy-to-make probiotic food, especially when you have a slow cooker on hand. Its slow, moist, steady heat is ideal for probiotic cultures, which thrive in this environment. Instead of hunting out yogurt starters, make it easy on yourself and use a good-quality commercial brand of yogurt (with no fruit or added sugar and preferably grass-fed) as a starter. Be sure to use a yogurt that is rich in active probiotic cultures like *L. bulgaricus* and *L. acidophilus*, *Bifidus* (look for these words on the label), because those cultures will multiply easily in warmed milk. Research has also shown that these particular cultures can lower cholesterol and help with allergies.

MAKES 8 CUPS [2 L]

8 cups [2 L] grass-fed whole milk

1 tsp ground turmeric

¼ tsp freshly ground black pepper

1 cup [240 ml] yogurt

Put the milk, turmeric, and pepper in the slow cooker and stir well. Cover the slow cooker and cook on the low setting for 2 to 2½ hours, until the milk is hot and starts to bubble around the edges. Turn the slow cooker off and leave covered. Let the milk cool to 110°F [43°C], about 30 minutes.

When the milk has cooled, gently stir in the yogurt just until incorporated. Unplug the slow cooker, then wrap the sides of the slow cooker with a small bath towel, using a rubber band to secure the towel. Let rest 8 to 12 hours, to allow the cultures to grow and multiply. The mixture will thicken but be looser than a store-bought yogurt. Serve immediately, or refrigerate in an airtight container for at least 1 hour to serve cold. Store the remaining yogurt in an airtight container in the refrigerator for up to 1 week.

Nutritional Stats per Serving

129 calories, 10 g protein, 17 g carbohydrates, 3 g fat (2 g saturated fat), 13 mg cholesterol, 13 g sugars, 2 g fiber, 113 mg sodium

PEPPER BERRY MILLET

The earthy flavor of black pepper mixed with raspberries instantly upgrades your morning porridge to a sweet and spicy treat. Lots of fiber from the berries feeds your good gut bugs, and the pepper enhances your body's ability to absorb antioxidants, such as the anthocyanins in raspberries, so that they stay in your body longer. Millet, an African grain that has a cornlike flavor, is rich in minerals like magnesium and contains a good dose of fiber to feed your gut.

SERVES 4

1 cup [180 g] millet

4 cups [480 g] fresh raspberries or sliced fresh strawberries

1 Tbsp grass-fed butter

1 tsp ground cinnamon

1 tsp freshly ground black pepper

One 1-in [2.5-cm] piece fresh ginger, peeled and minced

Pinch of cayenne pepper (optional)

Assorted fresh fruit for garnish

Put the millet, 4 cups [960 ml] water, raspberries, butter, cinnamon, black pepper, ginger, and cayenne (if using) in the slow cooker and stir well. Cover the slow cooker and cook on the low setting for 1½ to 2 hours, until most of the liquid is absorbed and the millet is tender.

Spoon into bowls and top with fresh fruit. Serve immediately.

Nutritional Stats per Serving
367 calories, 8 g protein, 53 g carbohydrates, 14 g fat (2 g saturated fat), 6 mg cholesterol, 6 g sugars, 14 g fiber, 10 mg sodium

BASIC BONE BROTH

Bone broth is a boon for digestive health since it can soothe delicate intestinal tissues and is very easy to digest. Once you make and taste this broth, you'll never go back to store-bought, since it takes slow-cooked meals from good to fabulous. Look for beef bones at a butcher shop or ask the butcher at your local grocery store for them, even if they aren't in the refrigerated section. I like to make a double batch of this culinary cornerstone and freeze it in several smaller containers so I have bone broth at the ready anytime I need it.

MAKES 4 QT [3.8 L] (SERVES 16)

1½ lb [680 g] grass-fed beef shank bones, marrow intact

1 onion, chopped

3 stalks celery, chopped

3 carrots, peeled and chopped

2 bay leaves

½ cup [6 g] fresh flat-leaf parsley stems and leaves

¼ cup [60 ml] apple cider vinegar

Pinch of salt

Put the bones, onion, celery, carrots, bay leaves, parsley, vinegar, and salt in the slow cooker. Pour water into the slow cooker until it reaches 1 inch [2.5 cm] below the rim. Cover the slow cooker and cook on the low setting for 6 to 6½ hours, until a fragrant broth forms and the bone marrow is cooked and starts to separate from the bone.

Strain the broth through a fine-mesh sieve, then scoop out the marrow from the bones and stir it into the strained broth. Discard the empty bones, vegetables, and other solids and allow the broth to cool to room temperature. Transfer to airtight containers and store in the refrigerator for up to 1 week or freeze for up to 6 months.

Nutritional Stats per Serving
67 calories, 5 g protein, 2 g carbohydrates, 2 g fat (2 g saturated fat), 0 mg cholesterol, 1 g sugars, 1 g fiber, 52 mg sodium

FRENCH ONION
BONE BROTH SOUP

In this soup, two of this chapter's healing ingredients, black pepper and bone broth, are paired with onion, a megastar for strengthening and detoxing your heart and blood vessels. Onion is rich in an antioxidant called quercetin, which is like a fertilizer for your microbiome, as it helps protect the growth of the good gut bugs. Keep much of the papery onion skin intact—it will become edible as it cooks.

SERVES 8

3 Tbsp grass-fed butter, at room temperature

2 lb [910 g] sweet onions, such as Vidalia

1 Tbsp Bragg Liquid Aminos or 2 Tbsp Worcestershire sauce

1 Tbsp black peppercorns

4 cups [960 ml] Basic Bone Broth (page 59)

1 Tbsp fresh thyme leaves or chopped rosemary

Rub the inside of the slow cooker with the butter. Peel the loose papery skins off the onions, leaving the thinner inner skins intact. Thinly slice the onions. Add the onions and the Bragg Liquid Aminos to the slow cooker and toss to coat. Cover the slow cooker and cook on the high setting for 4 hours, until the onions are very soft.

Put the peppercorns on a cutting board and, using a skillet, crush the peppercorns. Add the crushed peppercorns to the slow cooker, cover, and cook for 4 hours more, until the onions brown slightly and give off their liquid.

Add the broth and cook on the low setting for 30 minutes more to allow the flavors to meld. Stir in the thyme. If you like, discard the softened onion skins. Or spoon them along with the soup into bowls. Serve immediately.

CHEF'S NOTE: To make this recipe more filling, add 1 lb [455 g] cooked peeled, deveined medium shrimp or shredded cooked chicken, or ½ cup [40 g] shredded fresh mozzarella to the cooked soup.

Nutritional Stats per Serving
183 calories, 8 g protein, 14 g carbohydrates, 6 g fat (5 g saturated fat), 90 mg cholesterol, 6 g sugars, 3 g fiber, 267 mg sodium

STRAWBERRY BEET SOUP

This sweet yet earthy soup has a brilliant fuchsia hue that is a feast for your eyes as well as your taste buds. It combines all four of the healing ingredients in this chapter—black pepper, probiotic dairy (in the form of buttermilk), bone broth, and berries—so if you need a lot of rebuilding, this is the recipe to make. Beets are the "meat" of this soup and they add important B vitamins and folate, a must-have nutrient for your nervous system and to strengthen your heart. Hempseeds are high in vitamin E and iron and make a flavorful nutty garnish.

SERVES 8

2 lb [910 g] beets, peeled

4 cups [960 ml] Basic Bone Broth (page 59) or chicken broth

½ tsp salt

¼ tsp freshly ground black pepper

6 cups [720 g] fresh strawberries, hulled

1 cup [240 ml] buttermilk

¼ cup [30 g] hempseeds or ¼ cup [35 g] sesame seeds

Put the beets, broth, salt, and pepper in the slow cooker. Cover the slow cooker and cook on the high setting for 2 to 2½ hours, until the beets are fork-tender. Using an immersion blender, purée until smooth. Add the strawberries and purée again until smooth.

Spoon into bowls and top each serving with 2 Tbsp buttermilk and ½ Tbsp hempseeds. Serve immediately.

Nutritional Stats per Serving
227 calories, 12 g protein, 24 g carbohydrates, 5 g fat (2 g saturated fat), 2 mg cholesterol, 16 g sugars, 6 g fiber, 337 mg sodium

BRANZINO WITH OLIVES, GOJI BERRIES, AND MINT SALAD

Berries and fish? It may seem odd, but dried goji berries pair so nicely with this dish. I like to cook with branzino because it is a sustainable fish in the sea bass family; you can substitute any white fish you prefer, such as flounder. This is a recipe that not only helps improve your digestion but is light on calories. In traditional Chinese medicine, goji berries are used to tonify the liver and kidneys, but modern science prizes them since they rate high on the antioxidant scale. A recent study also showed that gojis may help with gastrointestinal function by soothing digestion.

SERVES 4

Eight 4-oz [115-g] skin-on branzino fillets

6 Tbsp [90 ml] extra-virgin olive oil

4 Tbsp [35 g] pitted black olives

1 tsp dried oregano

2 Tbsp red wine vinegar or balsamic vinegar

¼ tsp salt

¼ tsp freshly ground black pepper

10 oz [280 g] watercress or baby kale

1 cup [12 g] packed, whole fresh mint leaves

¼ cup [30 g] goji berries or ¼ cup [35 g] dried cherries

Lay 4 of the branzino fillets in the bottom of the slow cooker. Drizzle with 1 Tbsp of the oil and sprinkle with 2 Tbsp olives and the oregano. Top with the remaining fillets and drizzle with 1 Tbsp oil and the remaining 2 Tbsp olives. Cover the slow cooker and cook on the low setting for 1 to 1½ hours, until the fish flakes when pressed with a fork.

While the branzino cooks, prepare the salad. Whisk together the remaining 4 Tbsp [60 ml] olive oil, the vinegar, salt, and pepper in a large bowl. Add the watercress, mint, and goji berries and toss until the greens are evenly coated in the dressing. Divide the salad between four plates and top each with two branzino fillets. Serve immediately.

Nutritional Stats per Serving

249 calories, 25 g protein, 5 g carbohydrates, 14 g fat (2 g saturated fat), 53 mg cholesterol, 2 g sugars, 1 g fiber, 245 mg sodium

SCALLOPS
WITH BLUEBERRY SAUCE

This blueberry sauce made with balsamic perfectly complements the buttery mild scallops. It's a full-on nutritional win with prebiotic-rich carrots and onion, high-fiber blueberries, and mineral-rich scallops. Scallops are also high in vitamins like B12, an important nutrient for your nervous system, brain, and cardiovascular health. Look for "dry" scallops, which aren't treated with sodium tripolyphosphate, a preservative that can also make them stringy when cooked.

SERVES 4

1 lb [455 g] carrots, peeled and thinly sliced

One 12-oz [340-g] bag frozen peas, defrosted

1 onion, chopped

2 Tbsp grass-fed butter or coconut oil

½ tsp salt

½ tsp freshly ground black pepper

1 lb [455 g] sea scallops

½ tsp paprika

2 cups [280 g] fresh blueberries

2 Tbsp olive oil

2 Tbsp balsamic vinegar

1 garlic clove, chopped

Put the carrots, peas, onion, butter, ¼ tsp salt, and the pepper in the slow cooker and stir well. Season the scallops with the remaining ¼ tsp salt and the paprika. Place the scallops on top of the vegetables. Cover the slow cooker and cook on the low setting for 1 to 1½ hours, until the scallops are cooked through and are no longer translucent in the center; to check for doneness, slice a scallop in half to check the center.

While the scallops cook, put the blueberries, olive oil, vinegar, and garlic in a food processor and process until smooth.

Divide the vegetable mixture among four plates and top with the scallops. Drizzle the blueberry sauce over the scallops and serve immediately.

Nutritional Stats per Serving
391 calories, 24 g protein, 41 g carbohydrates, 14 g fat (5 g saturated fat), 15 mg cholesterol, 19 g sugars, 9 g fiber, 649 mg sodium

STRAWBERRY BALSAMIC SALMON WITH ASPARAGUS

If you love the flavors of teriyaki, then you'll be hooked on this dish, which uses berries mixed with balsamic vinegar, resulting in a sweet-and-sour sauce that's lovely on salmon. Strawberries are not only a superfood for your gut, but they also happen to be extremely high in vitamin C. If you choose to garnish this dish with antioxidant-rich hibiscus flowers (which you can buy on the Internet), be sure they are finely ground if you use them dry. If you have a whole dried hibiscus flower, rehydrate it in hot water for 15 minutes first and then slice it before using.

SERVES 4

1 lb [455 g] asparagus, trimmed and chopped

1 Tbsp extra-virgin olive oil

¼ cup [60 ml] balsamic vinegar

1 Tbsp honey

1 tsp red pepper flakes

¼ tsp salt

¼ tsp freshly ground black pepper

Four 4-oz [115-g] skin-on salmon fillets

1 lb [455 g] strawberries, diced

2 Tbsp ground dried hibiscus flowers or chopped fresh flat-leaf parsley or cilantro

Put the asparagus and oil in the slow cooker and toss until the asparagus is evenly coated. Whisk together the vinegar, honey, pepper flakes, salt, and black pepper in a small bowl. Place the salmon fillets skin-side down on top of the asparagus in the slow cooker. Drizzle with the vinegar mixture and sprinkle with the strawberries. Cover the slow cooker and cook on the low setting for 2 to 2½ hours, until the salmon flakes when pressed with a fork and the asparagus is tender.

Divide the asparagus among four plates and top each with a salmon fillet. Spoon the sauce over the top and sprinkle with the hibiscus. Serve immediately.

Nutritional Stats per Serving
366 calories, 27 g protein, 23 g carbohydrates, 19 g fat (4 g saturated fat), 62 mg cholesterol, 16 g sugars, 5 g fiber, 221 mg sodium

SHREDDED FLANK STEAK
AU POIVRE

This recipe is a combination of many good things: it uses bone broth, which is high in gut-healing gelatin; beef to boost iron; and warming, high-antioxidant black pepper. If you love French food but feel intimidated to cook it, here is a no-muss recipe that uses the same great flavors, and it's easily prepared in a slow cooker. Making this recipe with bone broth takes the intense flavor to a new level. If you must use a store-bought broth, opt for low-sodium beef broth since it relies on deeply roasted veggies and meat for flavor in lieu of high levels of salt. Salad makes the base instead of noodles and is a good way to get your greens!

SERVES 6

1½ lb [910 g] flank steak

2 cups [480 ml] Basic Bone Broth (page 59) or low-sodium beef broth or mushroom broth

2 sweet onions, such as Vidalia, chopped

4 garlic cloves, thinly sliced

1 Tbsp freshly ground black pepper

¼ cup [60 ml] half-and-half

2 Tbsp extra-virgin olive oil

2 Tbsp balsamic vinegar

¼ tsp seasoning salt

10 oz [280 g] mesclun or baby spinach

Put the flank steak, broth, onions, garlic, and pepper in the slow cooker. Cover the slow cooker and cook on the high setting for 5 to 6 hours, until the meat is very tender and shreds when pressed with a fork. Transfer the steak to a cutting board to cool for 10 minutes. Turn the slow cooker off. Shred the steak with two forks and return it to the slow cooker. Add the half-and-half and toss together until the steak and onions are evenly coated.

Whisk together the oil, vinegar, and seasoning salt in a large bowl. Add the mesclun and toss until evenly coated with the dressing.

Divide the mesclun among four plates and top with the shredded beef. Serve immediately.

Nutritional Stats per Serving
287 calories, 28 g protein, 10 g carbohydrates, 15 g fat (5 g saturated fat), 57 mg cholesterol, 3 g sugars, 2 g fiber, 266 mg sodium

TOMATO SPINACH BUFFALO MEATBALLS WITH CUCUMBER SALAD

Buffalo has the same meaty taste as beef and is one of the leanest meats around. Most grass-fed meats are leaner because the animals eat their greens instead of the grains that fatten up conventionally raised animals. Grass-fed meat contains seven times the amount of omega-3 fats compared with its corn-fed counterparts, making it a better choice for the health-conscious. Omega-3 fats, the super healer from the fat world, can help to prevent PMS, heart disease, and depression.

SERVES 6

1½ lb [680 g] ground buffalo or bison

3 cups [60 g] baby spinach, chopped

4 large eggs

¼ cup [55 g] tomato paste

½ cup [70 g] cornmeal or ½ cup [50 g] flaked quinoa

1 tsp garlic salt

1 tsp dried oregano

2 cups [480 ml] Basic Bone Broth (page 59) or chicken broth

CUCUMBER SALAD

3 lb [1.4 kg] cucumbers, peeled and thinly sliced

¼ tsp salt

½ cup [20 g] chopped fresh cilantro, dill, or basil

½ cup [120 ml] olive oil

¼ cup [60 ml] raw apple cider vinegar

½ red or yellow onion, thinly sliced

½ tsp freshly ground black pepper

Put the buffalo, spinach, eggs, tomato paste, cornmeal, garlic salt, and oregano in a large bowl and mix well with your fingers—the mixture will be sticky. Form into 36 small meatballs.

Transfer the meatballs to a slow cooker and pour in the broth. Cover the slow cooker and cook on the low setting for 2 to 2½ hours, stirring once or twice, until the meatballs are cooked through.

CONT'D

While the meatballs are cooking, make the cucumber salad. Place the cucumbers in a large colander, sprinkle with the salt, and let drain in the sink for 15 minutes. Squeeze the cucumbers with your hands to release any residual moisture and transfer to another large bowl. Add the cilantro, oil, vinegar, onion, and pepper and toss well.

Transfer the meatballs and salad to plates. Serve immediately.

———————————————————————

Nutritional Stats per Serving
527 calories, 35 g protein, 21 g carbohydrates, 32 g fat (8 g saturated fat), 186 mg cholesterol, 6 g sugars, 3 g fiber, 514 mg sodium

PEPPERY LAMB VINDALOO WITH CHERRIES

Have a chile addict in your house? Vindaloo is a traditional, blazing hot curry dish that's flavored with plenty of chiles and vinegar. This vindaloo is different from most in its class since it tosses in dried cherries and black pepper. Chiles and black pepper make a wonderful pair since they contain a few of the same health-promoting qualities, like helping your body burn calories at a higher rate and also working as a natural appetite suppressant.

SERVES 8

2 lb [910 g] lamb stew meat

1 lb [455 g] carrots, peeled and chopped

8 oz [230 g] green beans, cut into pieces

1 onion, chopped

1 cup [240 g] vindaloo curry paste

½ cup [70 g] dried cherries

1 Tbsp freshly ground black pepper

Put the lamb, ½ cup [120 ml] water, the carrots, green beans, onion, curry paste, cherries, and pepper in the slow cooker and toss until the vegetables are evenly coated in the paste. Cover the slow cooker and cook on the low setting for 3 to 3½ hours, until the lamb and vegetables are tender. Spoon the curry into eight bowls and serve immediately.

Nutritional Stats per Serving
307 calories, 25 g protein, 24 g carbohydrates, 15 g fat (2 g saturated fat), 73 mg cholesterol, 13 g sugars, 7 g fiber, 569 mg sodium

CIRCULATE AND STABILIZE

MEET THE INGREDIENTS:
Cinnamon, Spinach, Legumes, Basil,
Grass-Fed and Pasture-Raised Meats

CHAPTER 3
CIRCULATE AND STABILIZE

Strengthen Vascular System, Calm Heart

The heart of this chapter is the vascular system, which includes heart health, blood health, and how well your blood circulates to transport nutrients (in the form of amino acids and electrolytes), oxygen, carbon dioxide, hormones, and blood cells throughout the body. Reducing your cardiovascular risk is deeply linked to what you eat on a regular basis, and just a few improvements to your diet can make a big difference. You'll learn to feast on foods that help to build blood health and better circulation, rebalance cholesterol, and detox the heart and blood vessels. And you'll also learn to cook with foods that contain heart-healing compounds, such as cinnamon, nuts, and spinach. Key circulating and stabilizing foods in this chapter provide a broad range of nutrients to fuel a healthy heart, from iron to fiber, vitamins like A and C, and folic acid.

Cinnamon, Spinach, Legumes, Basil, Grass-Fed and Pasture-Raised Meats

Cinnamon

Calm

Surprisingly sweet cinnamon regulates blood sugar, since it improves glucose and lipid metabolism, as well as strengthening your blood capillaries. Keeping your blood sugar stable is important for your heart for two reasons: it's a simple way to control your weight and a smart preventative step for type 2 diabetes, which greatly increases your risk for cardiovascular disease.

Cinnamon also contains a powerful antioxidant called cinnamaldehyde that has been studied for its antimicrobial activity, which benefits the body and especially your gut bacteria that deal with immunity and have huge impact on the health of your heart by helping to control weight gain and insulin levels and ward off diabetes.

Spinach

Strengthen

Leafy greens are a staple in a heart-healthy diet since they contain essential nutrients (high levels of vitamins A, C, and B complex) that also happen to stop oxidative stress, one of the biggest problems for your heart. Think of it like rust on metal which causes clogs, or like holes created because of oxygen exposure inside pipes. This is, in a way, what happens to cells and tissues, and it's bad news since the heart (a.k.a. the pump) and the blood vessels (a.k.a. the plumbing or pipes) use blood to carry nutrients around the body.

Spinach is a standout green for heart health since it contains more folate, a B vitamin, compared with other greens—66 percent of your daily needs in just one cup. Keeping your folate levels high (which can get drained from stress and alcohol consumption) is heart smart because it keeps homocysteine in check, an amino acid that also happens to be a marker for cardiovascular disease. When homocysteine is high you are more prone to cell injury, which causes blood vessels to become inflamed.

Legumes
Calm

Simple, earthy beans may not seem like a glamorous superfood, but if you're concerned about the state of your heart they will soon become your heart's desire! Many varieties of beans, especially black beans, are as high in antioxidants as blueberries and contain high levels of fiber mixed with protein for a filling plant-based meal. Like spinach, beans are high in folate as well as a special compound that slows the way digestive enzymes turn starches into sugar. Why do you care? It means you can eat food that fills you up while burning more calories and storing less fat. You'll also experience fewer hunger pangs because your blood sugar is more balanced, sending fewer "hunger cues" to the brain and keeping you from excess snacking.

Basil
Strengthen

Herbs aren't just for gourmet cooking, they are also great for health buffs since they contain high levels of antibacterial compounds that help to detoxify your organs. Like most greens, basil is also high in vitamin K, the essential nutrient for proper blood clotting as well as bone health. If you've ever enjoyed a dish with pesto, you already know that basil is the ideal herb to eat in large quantities, since it has a mild taste and pairs beautifully with so many ingredients, including the heart-healing ingredients in this chapter, spinach and beans.

Grass-Fed and Pasture-Raised Meats

Strengthen

Meat may seem like a strange addition to this chapter, but recent studies show that grass-fed meats have some surprising health benefits. Grass-fed beef contains high levels of omega-3s, a nutrient that decreases inflammation and keeps plaque (deposits caused by cholesterol breakdown that clog blood vessels) from catching as it cycles through the bloodstream. Beef is also the absolute best way to restock your iron stores. About 25 percent of the female population is iron-deficient, which can lead to feeling drained and constantly fatigued. If you are iron-deficient, beef is better than a plant-based diet, because it contains a special form of iron called heme, which can be absorbed by the bloodstream up to 50 percent more than the iron from plants. Beef is also a rich source of vitamin B_{12}, which is vital for stabilizing iron levels (one of the goals of this chapter), since it's crucial for nearly all of our body's systems, including maintaining limber arteries and a calm, hearty nervous system.

HUEVOS RANCHEROS
WITH PINK PINTOS

Huevos rancheros (ranchers' eggs) is a hearty breakfast with roots in Mexico, where it was served to hardworking folk as a midmorning meal. It contains heart-healthy beans and filling, protein-rich eggs, making it ideal for a weekend brunch or a post-workout refuel. If you want a healthy variation, simply top half the eggs with jarred red tomato salsa and the other half with jarred green salsa or the leftover sauce from Chicken Basil Kale Verde (page 49). Most people are aware that beans are high in fiber and heart-healthy, but beans are also high in potassium, a mineral that helps to lower blood pressure by keeping sodium levels in check.

SERVES 8

One 14½-oz [411-g] can diced tomatoes

One 15-oz [425-g] can reduced-sodium pinto beans, drained and rinsed

½ onion, diced

2 garlic cloves, minced

5 oz [140 g] cooked chorizo sausage links, chopped

8 large eggs

1 tsp mild chili powder

½ tsp freshly ground black pepper

¼ tsp ground cumin (optional)

16 small corn tortillas

1 cup [80 g] shredded cheese, such as cheddar or mozzarella, or 1 cup [120 g] crumbled feta (optional)

2 avocados, peeled, pitted, and diced (optional)

Put the tomatoes, beans, onion, garlic, and chorizo in the slow cooker. Cover the slow cooker and cook on the low setting for 2 to 2½ hours, until the sauce thickens. Uncover the slow cooker, crack the eggs, and carefully place them over the bean and sauce mixture, spacing them evenly apart. Sprinkle the eggs with the chili powder, black pepper, and cumin (if using). Cover the slow cooker and cook on the low setting for 30 to 45 minutes more, until the egg whites are cooked through but the yolks are still soft.

CONT'D

Just before serving, warm the tortillas in a toaster oven or on a gas burner. For each serving, place 2 tortillas on a plate and top with the 2 heaping tablespoons of the bean mixture and 1 egg. Sprinkle with the cheese or avocado (if using). Serve immediately.

Nutritional Stats per Serving

334 calories, 20 g protein, 35 g carbohydrates, 14 g fat (6 g saturated fat), 223 mg cholesterol, 4 g sugars, 7 g fiber, 472 mg sodium

SMOKY HABANERO BAKED BEANS

Habaneros are the fiery hot fruit of a nightshade plant, and they're the ideal way to turn bland beans into a flavor fest, especially when paired with smoked sea salt. They come in multiple vibrant colors, ranging from green and orange to red and yellow. Beans are a grounding food that not only fill your belly with loads of fiber but may also help prevent metabolic syndrome (when your weight, metabolism, and cholesterol are completely out of balance). Beans also deliver a wide range of antioxidants in the form of tannins, phenolic acids, and flavonoids that reside in their fiber-rich skins. Basil's benefits reside in its volatile oils, like estragole and limonene, which are antibacterial and also give basil its wonderful fragrance.

SERVES 8

2 cups [360 g] dried navy beans, rinsed

1 onion, chopped

¼ cup [60 ml] Basic Bone Broth (page 59) or chicken broth

¼ cup [10 g] chopped fresh basil or cilantro

2 Tbsp molasses

2 Tbsp tomato paste

4 garlic cloves, minced

1 habanero chile, seeded and chopped

1 tsp smoked sea salt

Put the navy beans in the slow cooker and add enough water to just barely cover the beans. Cover the slow cooker and cook on the low setting for 3 to 3½ hours, until the beans are tender and most of the liquid is absorbed.

Add the onion, broth, basil, molasses, tomato paste, garlic, habanero, and sea salt. Cook on the low setting for 2 to 2½ hours more, until the sauce is thick and the beans are very soft.

Spoon the beans into bowls and serve immediately.

Nutritional Stats per Serving
198 calories, 12 g protein, 37 g carbohydrates, 1 g fat (0 g saturated fat), 0 mg cholesterol, 6 g sugars, 13 g fiber, 333 mg sodium

TWICE SLOW-COOKED CINNAMON BALSAMIC SWEET POTATO

These soulfully spiced sweet potatoes are satisfying enough to be a main dish, and they pack in two heart-healthy ingredients, vitamin A and fiber. Just add a side of greens for a nutritional boost, or a scoop of meaty leftovers, such as the Chicken Basil Kale Verde (page 49) or the Shredded Flank Steak au Poivre (page 69). Cinnamon is a healing spice with anti-diabetic properties, and even in small amounts (less than ¼ tsp daily), it has real benefits to help stabilize blood sugar.

SERVES 8

4 sweet potatoes

½ cup [120 ml] balsamic vinegar

4 Tbsp [55 g] grass-fed butter, at room temperature

2 Tbsp tomato paste

1 tsp mild chili powder

1 tsp ground cinnamon

½ tsp garlic salt

¼ tsp freshly ground black pepper

4 scallions, thinly sliced, green and white parts

½ cup [120 ml] maple syrup (optional)

Scrub the sweet potatoes, but do not dry them, then put them in the slow cooker. Add 1 Tbsp water, cover the slow cooker, and cook on the high setting for 2½ to 3 hours, until the potatoes are tender. Transfer the potatoes to a cutting board.

Cut the sweet potatoes in half lengthwise. Scoop out the flesh, reserving the skins to refill and being careful not to tear the skins while you scoop out the flesh. Put the sweet potato flesh, vinegar, butter, tomato paste, chili powder, cinnamon, garlic salt, and pepper in a large bowl and stir until combined.

CONT'D

Place the potato skins skin-side down in the slow cooker and fill with the sweet potato mixture, dividing the mixture evenly among the skins. Sprinkle the scallions over the top. Cover the slow cooker and cook on the high heat setting for about 30 minutes, until warmed through. Transfer to a plate and serve immediately, drizzled with syrup, if using.

Nutritional Stats per Serving

250 calories, 2 g protein, 47 g carbohydrates, 5 g fat (4 g saturated fat), 15 mg cholesterol, 22 g sugars, 4 g fiber, 179 mg sodium

LAYERED LENTIL ENCHILADA WITH SPINACH SALAD

Lentils are rich in the little-known antioxidant molybdenum, which is important for regulating several enzymes in our body. Molybdenum is critical for keeping healing sulfur compounds (like the ones you'll find in kale and other cruciferous vegetables) in your body for better detox. Think of herbs, like basil, as detox flavor helpers, since they all contain antibacterial compounds without adding anything extra that can block healing like sugar, preservatives, or high levels of salt.

SERVES 6

2 cups [400 g] red lentils

2 cups [480 ml] Basic Bone Broth (page 59) or chicken broth

2 garlic cloves, minced

2 Tbsp mild chili powder

½ tsp ground cumin

½ tsp freshly ground black pepper

One 14-oz [396-g] can enchilada sauce

4 corn tortillas

1 cup [80 g] shredded cheese, such as cheddar or mozzarella, or 1 cup [120 g] crumbled feta

5 oz [140 g] baby spinach

1 cup [20 g] packed fresh basil leaves

1 Tbsp olive oil

1 Tbsp apple cider vinegar

Put the lentils, broth, garlic, chili powder, cumin, and pepper in the slow cooker. Cover the slow cooker and cook on the low setting for 1 to 1½ hours, until the lentils are tender and most of the liquid is absorbed.

Spoon out half of the lentils and transfer them to a plate. Drizzle half of the enchilada sauce on top of the lentils that are in the slow cooker. Layer 2 tortillas on top of the lentils in the slow cooker. Return the remaining lentils from the plate to the slow cooker and top with the 2 remaining tortillas. Drizzle with the remaining enchilada sauce and sprinkle with the cheese. Cover the slow cooker and cook on the low setting for 30 minutes, until the cheese has melted and the tortillas are soft.

CONT'D

Just before serving, put the spinach, basil, oil, and vinegar in a large bowl and toss until the greens are evenly coated.

Divide the spinach salad among 6 plates. Using a small knife or the sharp edge of a spatula, divide the enchiladas into 6 portions and serve immediately alongside the salad.

Nutritional Stats per Serving

389 calories, 25 g protein, 52 g carbohydrates, 9 g fat (4 g saturated fat), 21 mg cholesterol, 2 g sugars, 21 g fiber, 376 mg sodium

CREAMY CINNAMON MILLET

Cinnamon is a superfood that balances blood sugar, since it's rich in manganese, a mineral that your body needs to properly process sugars. If you don't have mango or pear, leftover poached pears (page 33) are a delightful fruit pairing with this warming breakfast bowl. Grass-fed butter not only makes this millet creamy and more flavorful and filling, but it also ramps up the omega-3 fats. Sneaking in turmeric is always a good idea because it has so many healing properties and is easy to sprinkle on top of almost any dish. Use it as a garnish here.

SERVES 4

1 cup [180 g] millet

1 Tbsp grass-fed butter

2 tsp ground cinnamon

½ tsp freshly grated nutmeg

¼ tsp freshly ground black pepper

Pinch of cayenne pepper (optional)

¼ cup [60 g] mascarpone or coconut cream

2 cups [310 g] diced mango or 2 cups [320 g] diced pears

½ tsp ground turmeric

Put the millet, 4 cups [960 ml] water, the butter, cinnamon, nutmeg, black pepper, and cayenne (if using) in the slow cooker and stir well. Cover the slow cooker and cook on the low setting for 1½ to 2 hours, until most of the liquid is absorbed and the grains are tender. Stir in the mascarpone.

Spoon into bowls and top with the mango. Sprinkle with the turmeric and serve immediately.

Nutritional Stats per Serving

367 calories, 8 g protein, 53 g carbohydrates, 14 g fat (2 g saturated fat), 6 mg cholesterol, 6 g sugars, 14 g fiber, 10 mg sodium

MISO SALMON

Miso, a mouth-watering fermented soybean paste, can turn plain salmon into an instant restaurant-quality gourmet dish. Salmon, like beef, is a great source of B_{12}, which is important not only for keeping your arteries healthy but also to help with the absorption of omega-3s. You'll also find good levels of vitamin D—which helps regulate blood sugar—in salmon, and wild salmon is an even better source than the farmed-raised version. Beans and spinach, two high-fiber foods that are both loaded with antioxidants, make the filling base for this savory fish.

SERVES 4

1 Tbsp Asian sesame oil

One 15-oz [425-g] can reduced-sodium black beans, drained and rinsed

1 bunch spinach, stemmed and chopped

Four 4-oz [115-g] skin-on salmon fillets

2 Tbsp white miso

2 garlic cloves, minced

One 1-in [2.5-cm] piece fresh ginger, peeled and minced

Rub the inside of the slow cooker with the oil. Add the beans, spinach, and 2 Tbsp cold water and toss well. Place the salmon fillets skin-side down on top of the bean mixture. In a small bowl, stir together the miso, garlic, ginger, and 2 Tbsp of water until a smooth paste forms. Spoon the miso mixture over the salmon.

Cover the slow cooker and cook on the low setting for 45 to 60 minutes, until the salmon flakes when pressed with a fork.

Transfer the salmon to plates and serve immediately with the spinach and beans on the side.

Nutritional Stats per Serving
364 calories, 30 g protein, 21 g carbohydrates, 19 g fat (4 g saturated fat), 62 mg cholesterol, 2 g sugars, 7 g fiber, 654 mg sodium

PINCH OF CINNAMON BOLOGNESE

A traditional Bolognese sauce requires three cooking techniques: searing, sweating, and braising. Using your slow cooker is a tasty shortcut that still yields a tender, flavorful ragù. Cinnamon adds an unexpected hint of sweetness, and this healing spice also contains cinnamaldehyde and cinnamic acid, which are both cardioprotective. Grass-fed and pasture-raised farm animals graze on green plants, which changes the makeup of their meat, meaning that it contains more beta-carotene, vitamin E, and omega-3s than their grain-fed counterparts.

SERVES 6

1 lb [455 g] grass-fed beef stew meat

2 bone-in pasture-raised pork chops, about 8 oz [230 g] total

1 onion, chopped

4 carrots, peeled and grated

2 celery stalks, thinly sliced

4 garlic cloves, minced

One 14½-oz [411-g] can diced tomatoes

¼ cup [55 g] tomato paste

1 tsp dried oregano or ½ tsp chopped fresh oregano

½ tsp salt

½ tsp freshly ground black pepper

¼ tsp ground cinnamon

1 lb [455 g] gluten-free pasta

½ cup [15 g] grated Parmesan

Put the beef, pork chops, onion, carrots, celery, garlic, diced tomatoes, tomato paste, oregano, salt, pepper, and cinnamon in the slow cooker. Cover the slow cooker and cook on the high setting for 4 to 4½ hours, until the beef and pork are fork-tender and start to fall apart.

Just before the beef and pork is ready, bring a large pot of salted water to a boil. Add the pasta and cook according to the package instructions. Drain and set aside.

CONT'D

Shred the beef and pork with two forks, discarding the bones. Return the shredded meat to the slow cooker and toss with the sauce until well coated. Add the pasta and toss until well coated.

Spoon into bowls and serve immediately with the Parmesan for passing at the table.

Nutritional Stats per Serving

469 calories, 33 g protein, 51 g carbohydrates, 8 g fat (3 g saturated fat), 56 mg cholesterol, 8 g sugars, 5 g fiber, 537 mg sodium

CHICKPEA CAULIFLOWER KORMA

Don't digest beans well, but still want to include them in your meals? Chickpeas are your best bet, since they are low in FODMAPS (an acronym for fermentable sugars) that are hard for those with digestive issues to process. If you love Indian takeout but not the caloric overload from lots of frying oil and too much heavy cream, make a lighter version that's just as tasty in your slow cooker. You can find korma curry paste at international grocery stores or online at places like Amazon.com or iShopIndian.com.

SERVES 6

1 large head cauliflower, about 2½ lb [1.2 kg], cut into florets

One 15-oz [425-g] can chickpeas, drained and rinsed

One 14½-oz [411-g] can diced tomatoes

1 cup [40 g] chopped fresh cilantro

1 small onion, diced

4 garlic cloves, minced

One 1-in [2.5-cm] piece fresh ginger, peeled and minced

2 cups [560 g] korma curry sauce

Put the cauliflower, chickpeas, tomatoes, cilantro, onion, garlic, ginger, and curry sauce in the slow cooker and toss until everything is evenly coated in the sauce. Cover the slow cooker and cook on the low setting for 3 to 3½ hours, until the cauliflower is tender. Spoon into bowls and serve immediately.

Nutritional Stats per Serving

191 calories, 8 g protein, 29 g carbohydrates, 7 g fat (2 g saturated fat), 7 mg cholesterol, 14 g sugars, 9 g fiber, 617 mg sodium

PAPRIKA-DRENCHED GOULASH

Traditional stews like Hungarian goulash make great use of inexpensive, tougher cuts of meat and are a great way to get iron in a low-fat, low-calorie way. Grass-fed beef contains more than just good levels of omega-3s; you'll also find lots of B6 (needed for red blood cell production) as well as CLA (conjugated linoleic acid), which reduces risk of heart attack. Basil calms blood vessels, an added boon for your heart.

SERVES 8

2 lb [910 g] grass-fed beef stew meat

1 tsp salt

¼ cup [30 g] oat flour or ¼ cup [35 g] cornmeal

3 Tbsp paprika

1 tsp freshly ground black pepper

8 carrots, peeled and chopped

2 onions, diced

1 cup [240 ml] Basic Bone Broth (page 59) or low-sodium beef broth

½ cup [10 g] packed fresh basil leaves

Zest of 2 lemons

½ cup [120 g] sour cream or ½ cup [120 g] plain Greek yogurt

Put the beef in a bowl and sprinkle with the salt. Place the oat flour, paprika, and pepper on a wide plate and mix together with your fingertips. Dredge the beef in the flour mixture and then put in the slow cooker. Add the carrots and onions to the slow cooker and pour in the broth. Cover the slow cooker and cook on the low setting for 2½ to 3 hours, until the beef is fork-tender.

Spoon into bowls. Sprinkle with the basil and lemon zest. Serve immediately with the sour cream for passing at the table.

CHEF'S NOTE: If you don't have sour cream on hand, you can always serve goulash with plain, protein-rich Greek yogurt.

Nutritional Stats per Serving
249 calories, 27 g protein, 13 g carbohydrates, 9 g fat (3 g saturated fat), 81 mg cholesterol, 5 g sugars, 3 g fiber, 320 mg sodium

SHREDDED CINNAMON BEEF CHILI WITH BLACK BEANS

Are your nerves frayed? Get your beef on. It turns out that beef contains high levels of a supernutrient that's great for your nervous system, B_{12}. It supports two feel-good neurotransmitters (serotonin and dopamine) that are part of a healthy nervous system—which, in turn, help your nerves communicate smoothly with your brain and bring you a sense of calm and clarity. Adding antioxidant- and fiber-rich beans to beef helps to stabilize further, since beans contain fiber that beef can't deliver, meaning your gut bugs and immunity are better protected, while more antioxidants mean your organs and tissues are less inflamed—a further state of calm. For bigger appetites, serve with a simple spinach salad or a scoop of the Creamy Cinnamon Millet (page 89).

SERVES 8

2 lb [910 g] grass-fed beef stew meat

One 14½-oz [411-g] can diced tomatoes

One 15-oz [425-g] can black beans, drained and rinsed

2 Tbsp tomato paste

1 Tbsp chopped chipotle chiles in adobo or 2 Tbsp mild chili powder

½ tsp ground cinnamon

½ tsp freshly ground black pepper

Put the beef, diced tomatoes, beans, tomato paste, chipotle, cinnamon, and black pepper in the slow cooker and stir together. Cook on the high setting for 4 to 4½ hours, until the beef is fork-tender.

With a slotted spoon or tongs, transfer the beef to a work surface and let cool, 5 to 10 minutes. Shred the beef with two forks and return the shredded meat to the slow cooker and toss with the sauce until well coated.

Spoon into bowls and serve immediately.

Nutritional Stats per Serving

222 calories, 29 g protein, 14 g carbohydrates, 6 g fat (2 g saturated fat), 75 mg cholesterol, 3 g sugars, 4 g fiber, 234 mg sodium

SHARPEN AND REWIRE

MEET THE INGREDIENTS:
Chocolate, Apples, Nuts and Seeds,
Seafood, Cloves

SHARPEN AND REWIRE

Energize and Cleanse the Brain

Suffering from brain fog, scattered thoughts, and slow memory? Don't just blame it on getting older or being stressed—it could be the result of an undernourished brain. Research shows that a healthy, sharp brain is a well-fed brain, and certain foods are paramount to brain function. How do specific nutrients boost your brain? Vitamin B_{12} and iron help clearer thinking; vitamin C is responsible in taking out the garbage, or toxins, in your brain; and vitamin E and omega-3 fatty acids protect delicate brain tissues. And when it comes to regeneration, researchers now know that adult brains do in fact grow new brain cells! A protein called brain-derived neurotrophic factor (BDNF) is the key to regrowth. Zinc, magnesium, and many phytonutrients found in foods throughout this book, and specifically in this chapter, have a positive impact on BDNF. Apart from the science of brain food, eating your way to a sharper brain can also be a pleasure, since many of the top brain foods, including chocolate (hooray!), seafood, nuts, seeds, and spices, are also incredibly delicious.

Chocolate, Apples, Nuts and Seeds, Seafood, Cloves

Chocolate

Energize

Historically, chocolate—the bitter cacao bean, not the sugary candy we eat today—was prized as a potent medicinal food by both the Aztecs and the Spanish medical society of the 1600s. Used for centuries as a multi-purpose cure—for everything from clearer thinking to better libido—modern medical research now substantiates what Montezuma already knew, that chocolate is beneficial for both brain and body. Chocolate gets its power from flavonols, a type of flavonoid antioxidant that resides in the pigment of plants.

Apples

Energize

Apples, especially their skins, are high in quercetin, a flavonoid that helps neural cells dispel toxins. Studies on apple juice suggest that compounds in apples may improve the way neurotransmitters work, so that your brain cells relay messages faster to the body and you can feel and function better. Apples also benefit the microbiome (also called the second brain, because it contains even more neurons), which helps to determine how smoothly we process information as well as the quality of our moods. Foods like apples, rich in both pectin and fiber, feed the microbiome and make for smoother cruising on the gut-brain highway.

Nuts and Seeds

Cleanse

Magnesium, a super mineral that can help with nerve and brain-cell function, also speeds the recovery of our cells as we age by removing toxins and encouraging the healthy production of DNA. It's stored in your body and gets depleted quickly when our stress response is triggered. Doctors say that almost everyone is mildly deficient in

101

magnesium, and people who are really deficient suffer from anxiety, depression, and sleeplessness. Nuts and seeds are also rich in zinc, an important mineral for detox since it improves immunity, repairs cell damage, and plays a big role in hormone balance.

Seafood
Cleanse

The reason seafood is highlighted in this chapter is because it's chock-full of brain-charging nutrients that can help rewire your brain and sharpen your focus. High levels of B_{12} can be found in shellfish, the presence of which correlates to more brain cells, and salmon is rich in omega-3 fatty acids, which fight depression and also improve cognition for aging brains. Opt for low-mercury and sustainable seafood choices by following our recommendations in the recipes that follow. You can also consult the Seafood Watch from the Monterey Bay Aquarium for other sustainable suggestions if you want more variety.

Cloves
Energize

This perky spice, the dried flower bud of a tree, is incredibly high in manganese, one of the top brain foods. Manganese helps to protect the receptors that brain cells use to communicate and aids in creating energy in the body. Deficiency in both manganese and magnesium are quite common, so pair this flavorful bud with magnesium-rich foods like nuts and seeds.

CHOCOLATE-ALMOND QUINOA BREAKFAST WITH RASPBERRIES

It's easy to burn grains on the stove top, so you'll love this foolproof way to make them tender and tasty every time. Cloves lend dimension and interest to a chocolaty cereal that's almost double the fiber, protein, and antioxidants compared with the same serving of traditional chocolate-flavored hot cereals. Though technically a seed, quinoa is cooked and treated as a grain and it contains nutrients that can rewire your brain, such as magnesium, which helps to "relax" the GABA receptors that inhibit feel-good neurotransmitters like serotonin. Clove is not only a delightful spice to pair with seeds and nuts, but it contains a high amount of magnesium.

SERVES 8

2 cups [360 g] white or red quinoa, rinsed well under cold water

⅓ cup [25 g] unsweetened 100% cacao powder

2 Tbsp honey or 2 tsp stevia

½ tsp almond extract

½ tsp vanilla extract

¼ tsp ground cloves or 4 whole cloves

2 cups [240 g] fresh or frozen raspberries

1 cup [120 g] chopped toasted almonds

Put the quinoa, 5 cups [1.2 L] water, cacao powder, honey, almond extract, vanilla, and cloves in the slow cooker and stir well. Cover the slow cooker and cook on the low setting for 2 to 2½ hours, until the quinoa is tender. During the last 30 minutes of cooking, stir in ¼ to ½ cup [60 to 120 ml] water if the mixture becomes too dry.

Spoon into bowls and top with the raspberries and toasted almonds and serve immediately.

Nutritional Stats per Serving

299 calories, 11 g protein, 41 g carbohydrates, 12 g fat (1 g saturated fat), 0 mg cholesterol, 6 g sugars, 6 g fiber, 10 mg sodium

CHOCOLATE COCONUT BAKED APPLES

Worried that burning the candle at both ends will burn out your brain cells? Then load up on apples and chocolate—two brain-sharpening foods that taste great together and make a great breakfast, particularly if you like something sweet in the morning! Brain benefits come from nonessential nutrients like quercetin, which hides out in the peel of the humble apple, and epicatechin, an antioxidant found in chocolate's tannins. All nuts are great for your brain since they contain healthy fats, but walnuts are particularly good since they contain the highest levels of omega-3s.

SERVES 4

4 apples, such as Gala or Pink Lady

¼ cup [30 g] chopped walnuts or chopped almonds

¼ cup [20 g] unsweetened shredded coconut

2 Tbsp unsweetened 100% cacao powder

2 Tbsp brown sugar or 2 tsp stevia

½ tsp ground cinnamon

¼ tsp ground cloves

4 Tbsp grass-fed butter, cut into 4 slices

Use a melon baller or paring knife to hollow out the center of the apples, removing the core and the seeds but leaving the bottom of the apples intact. You should have a hollow about ½ inch wide and 2½ inches deep. Place the apples in the slow cooker. Stir together the walnuts, coconut, cacao powder, brown sugar, cinnamon, and cloves in a bowl. Spoon the nut mixture into the cavities of the apples and top each with a slice of butter. Cover the slow cooker and cook on the low setting for 3 to 3½ hours, until the apples are tender.

Transfer the apples to serving plates and serve immediately.

CHEF'S NOTE: If you're working with a round 3½-quart slow cooker, this recipe is easy to cut in half, and you can stack the apples on top of each other after they are stuffed. You may need to decrease the cooking time by 15 to 30 minutes.

Nutritional Stats per Serving (with brown sugar)
217 calories, 2 g protein, 33 g carbohydrates, 11 g fat (5 g saturated fat), 0 mg cholesterol, 24 g sugars, 6 g fiber, 5 mg sodium

Nutritional Stats per Serving (with stevia)
200 calories, 2 g protein, 30 g carbohydrates, 11 g fat (5 g saturated fat), 0 mg cholesterol, 19 g sugars, 6 g fiber, 4 mg sodium

SPICED CHOCOLATE NUTS

Nuts are well known for their benefits to heart health, but did you know that they are also a boon for your brain? Brain-boosting nuts include plenty of noninflammatory fats and vitamin E for better cognitive and memory performance, as well as manganese and omega-3s. Chocolate is a brain-beneficial food for many reasons. For one, dark chocolate can calm high blood pressure, which can impair cognitive ability and be very dangerous for your brain.

MAKES 4 CUPS [560 G] (SERVES 16)

Olive oil cooking spray

¼ cup [60 ml] maple syrup or agave syrup

2 Tbsp grass-fed butter, at room temperature, or coconut oil

⅓ cup [25 g] unsweetened 100% cacao powder

2 tsp vanilla extract

½ tsp salt

½ tsp ground cloves

⅛ tsp cayenne pepper

2 cups [280 g] whole almonds or walnut halves

2 cups [280 g] whole cashews or macadamia nuts

Line a slow cooker with aluminum foil and coat with cooking spray.

Stir together the maple syrup, butter, cacao powder, vanilla, salt, cloves, and cayenne in a large bowl. Add the almonds and cashews and toss until evenly coated. Transfer the nuts to the slow cooker, cover, and cook on the high setting for 1 hour. Turn the setting to low and cook, stirring once or twice during cooking, for 2 to 2½ hours more, until the cacao powder coating becomes dry and the nuts start to brown.

Cool completely and store in an airtight container at room temperature for up to 1 week. Or transfer to a large zipper-lock bag and freeze for up to 6 months.

Nutritional Stats per Serving

227 calories, 5 g protein, 9 g carbohydrates, 19 g fat (3 g saturated fat), 7 mg cholesterol, 4 g sugars, 3 g fiber, 74 mg sodium

CAULIFLOWER RICE WITH BUTTERMILK AND CACAO NIBS

Cauliflower "rice" is nothing more than cauliflower that's been cut into rice-size bits. When cooked, cauliflower rice has a similar texture to rice and also a whole lot more nutrition, like a high amount of vitamin C and liver-healing sulfur compounds. Chocolate may seem like a bizarre combo with cauliflower, but rich-tasting cacao nibs (cracked whole cacao beans) work well with savory dishes and add a pleasant crunch. Cacao nibs in small quantities provide big nutrition, including high levels of protein, fiber, and brain-healing fat, which helps to protect genes responsible for synaptic function (how brain cells talk to each other).

SERVES 6

1 large head cauliflower, about 2½ lb [1.2 kg], cut into florets

2 Tbsp grass-fed butter, at room temperature, or coconut oil

1 cup [240 ml] buttermilk

2 Tbsp mayonnaise

2 Tbsp apple cider vinegar

½ tsp garlic salt

½ tsp freshly ground black pepper

8 scallions, chopped, green and white parts

½ cup [60 g] cacao nibs

Working in batches, put the cauliflower florets in a food processor and pulse until the pieces resemble the size of rice kernels. Transfer the cauliflower to the slow cooker, add the butter, and toss until combined. Cover the slow cooker and cook on the low setting for 2 to 2½ hours, until the cauliflower is tender. Transfer to a large platter.

Whisk together the buttermilk, mayonnaise, vinegar, garlic salt, and pepper in a medium bowl and drizzle over the cauliflower. Sprinkle the scallions and cacao nibs over the top. Serve immediately.

Nutritional Stats per Serving
212 calories, 5 g protein, 14 g carbohydrates, 15 g fat (8 g saturated fat), 13 mg cholesterol, 5 g sugars, 5 g fiber, 238 mg sodium

CHILI-CHOCOLATE BLACK BEANS WITH CHORIZO

If you're tired of overly sweet baked beans, opt for this sassy take on a fiber-rich side dish. It's great to serve as a side for your favorite *Healing Slow Cooker* grain dish like Balsamic Goji Oats (page 127) or alongside scrambled eggs for a satisfying brunch. When it comes to healthy chocolate, only dark chocolate fits the bill, and unsweetened cacao powder is 100 percent of the good stuff. Just 1 tablespoon of cacao powder contains a day's worth of fiber and 4 percent of your RDA for iron.

SERVES 8

Two 15-oz [425-g] cans reduced-sodium black beans, drained and rinsed

8 oz [230 g] cooked chorizo sausage links, sliced

One 14½-oz [411-g] can diced tomatoes

2 red or green bell peppers, seeded, deribbed, and chopped

1 onion, diced

2 Tbsp unsweetened 100% cacao powder

1 Tbsp mild chili powder

1 tsp dried oregano

¼ tsp ground turmeric

¼ tsp freshly ground black pepper

Put the beans, chorizo, tomatoes, bell peppers, onion, cacao powder, chili powder, oregano, turmeric, and pepper in the slow cooker and stir well. Cover the slow cooker and cook on the low setting for 1 to 1½ hours, until the beans are hot and the flavors meld. Spoon into bowls and serve immediately.

Nutritional Stats per Serving

153 calories, 10 g protein, 26 g carbohydrates, 3 g fat (2 g saturated fat), 16 mg cholesterol, 5 g sugars, 8 g fiber, 534 mg sodium

CILANTRO-JALAPEÑO SHELLFISH CHOWDER

Hot spices mellow in coconut milk, the perfect sweet yet fatty liquid that aids in absorption of fat-soluble nutrients. Cooking spices in fat also helps to protect and deliver their active compounds. Shellfish, like mussels and clams, are an incredibly efficient way to nourish your brain because they contain high levels of so many brain chargers like B_{12} (wards off depression and anxiety), manganese and magnesium (both lower stress response), iron (protects against mood disorders), and zinc (allows brain cells to signal properly for health cognition).

SERVES 6

2 lb [910 g] mussels

1 lb [455 g] Manila clams

One 14-oz [420-ml] can full-fat coconut milk

2 shallots, thinly sliced

1 jalapeño chile, seeded and thinly sliced

1 Tbsp curry powder

¼ tsp salt

¼ tsp freshly ground black pepper

½ cup [20 g] chopped fresh cilantro

Rinse the mussels and clams in a colander under cold running water, pulling off any debris from the shells and discarding any that are open or have broken shells. Set aside.

Put the coconut milk, 1 cup [240 ml] water, shallots, jalapeño, curry powder, salt, and pepper in the slow cooker. Cover the slow cooker and cook on the high setting for 1 to 1½ hours, until the milk is hot and the spices are fragrant.

Add the mussels, clams, and cilantro. Cover the slow cooker and cook on the low setting for 2 to 2½ hours, until the shellfish open and are cooked through. Transfer the mussels to bowls and spoon over the sauce, discarding any shellfish that didn't open. Serve immediately.

Nutritional Stats per Serving
314 calories, 31 g protein, 12 g carbohydrates, 19 g fat (14 g saturated fat), 65 mg cholesterol, 1 g sugars, 0 g fiber, 566 mg sodium

ORANGE-CHIPOTLE SHRIMP IN BUTTER LETTUCE CUPS

Delicate, practically fat-free shrimp is ideal for the slow cooker, since gentle moist cooking won't dry out this lean protein. Shrimp delivers loads of B_{12} to your brain but also includes selenium, an antioxidant mineral that protects your thyroid and helps with hair growth. Just four ounces of shrimp gives you more than 100 percent of your daily recommended dose of selenium in a low-cal, tasty way.

SERVES 8

4 oranges

2 lb [910 g] peeled, deveined medium shrimp

1 bunch asparagus, trimmed and cut into thirds

One 28-oz [794-g] can diced tomatoes

2 Tbsp chopped chipotle chiles in adobo

2 Tbsp tomato paste

2 Tbsp coconut oil or grass-fed butter

1 tsp red pepper flakes

16 butter lettuce leaves

¼ cup [10 g] chopped fresh flat-leaf parsley or cilantro

2 avocados, peeled, pitted, and diced

Zest the oranges and set aside the zest.

Using a chef's knife, cut the peel from the oranges. To segment the oranges, work over a large bowl. Holding the peeled orange in your hand, use a small paring knife to slice between the white membranes of the orange to free the segments and allow them to drop into the bowl as you continue onto the next segment. Repeat with the remaining oranges. Set aside.

Put the shrimp, orange zest, asparagus, diced tomatoes, chipotles, tomato paste, coconut oil, and red pepper flakes in the slow cooker and toss well. Cover the slow cooker and cook on the low setting for 1½ hours, until the shrimp are cooked through and no longer translucent when sliced through with a knife.

Lay out the lettuce leaves on a platter. Spoon the shrimp into lettuce leaves and top with the orange segments, parsley, and avocado. Serve immediately.

Nutritional Stats per Serving
310 calories, 27 g protein, 24 g carbohydrates, 12 g fat (4 g saturated fat), 172 mg cholesterol, 8 g sugars, 8 g fiber, 244 mg sodium

PEPITA-LIME FISH TACOS

Pepitas is a Spanish word that refers to the shelled oval seeds from pumpkins. These little green gems deliver many minerals that keep your brain alert, including zinc (for memory), magnesium (helps neurons communicate), and manganese (wards off dementia), making them a superfood for your neurons. Getting healthy levels of these minerals can rewire the way your brain communicates with your body, since they not only help to safeguard the well-being of your neurons but are also essential to allowing neurons to pass messages effectively. Fish, a delicious flaky base for pepitas, rounds out this tidy list of protective nutrients by including B_{12} (healthy red blood cells), iodine, and selenium (both protective for your thyroid).

SERVES 4

2 cups [40g] packed baby spinach leaves

2 cups [40g] packed fresh cilantro stems and leaves

Zest and juice of 3 limes

½ cup [70 g] shelled pumpkin seeds

1 Tbsp olive oil

½ tsp salt

¼ tsp freshly ground black pepper

1 lb [455 g] halibut or pollack fillets

12 corn tortillas

2 cups [120 g] thinly sliced cabbage

1 cup [240 ml] tomato salsa

Put the spinach, cilantro, lime zest and juice, pumpkin seeds, oil, salt, and pepper in a food processor and pulse 10 to 15 times, until a chunky sauce forms. Spread the spinach-lime sauce over the top of the fillets and transfer to the slow cooker. Cover the slow cooker and cook on the low setting for 1½ to 2 hours, until the fish flakes when pressed with a fork.

Just before serving, warm the tortillas in a toaster oven or on a gas burner. Arrange the tortillas on a large patter. Divide the fish among the 12 tortillas and top with the cabbage and salsa. Serve immediately.

Nutritional Stats per Serving
411 calories, 31 g protein, 40 g carbohydrates, 16 g fat (2 g saturated fat), 55 mg cholesterol, 3 g sugars, 6 g fiber, 400 mg sodium

LEMON GINGER SCALLOPS OVER COCONUT PUMPKIN PURÉE

Scallops are treasures from the sea, and just four ounces will give you brain-enhancing nutrients such as B12 and choline, which is a mood enhancer. Choline not only helps you to look on the bright side, but this water-soluble nutrient also assists with nerve signaling, growth of brain tissues, and even proper liver function.

SERVES 6

One 15-oz [425-g] can 100% pure pumpkin purée

1 cup [240 ml] full-fat coconut milk

½ tsp salt

2 Tbsp grated fresh ginger

½ tsp ground turmeric

½ tsp mild chili powder

¼ tsp freshly ground black pepper

Zest of 1 lemon

2 lb [910 g] scallops

1 Tbsp coconut oil, melted

½ cup [60 g] goji berries

Stir together the pumpkin purée, coconut milk, and ¼ tsp of the salt in a large bowl, then pour into the slow cooker.

In a small bowl, stir together the remaining ¼ tsp salt, ginger, turmeric, chili powder, pepper, and lemon zest. On a plate, sprinkle both sides of the scallops with the ginger mixture. Place the scallops on top of the pumpkin mixture and drizzle with the coconut oil.

Cover the slow cooker and cook on the low setting for 2 to 2½ hours, until the scallops are cooked through and the pumpkin mixture is hot.

Transfer the scallops to plates and spoon the purée alongside them. Sprinkle with the goji berries and serve immediately.

Nutritional Stats per Serving

329 calories, 23 g protein, 23 g carbohydrates, 17 g fat (13 g saturated fat), 0 mg cholesterol, 10 g sugars, 4 g fiber, 523 mg sodium

GRASS-FED STROGANOFF WITH CACAO POWDER

Creating a rich gravy without browning meat or using a gluten-rich flour can be a challenge. But here, unsweetened cacao powder—rich in iron and antioxidants—helps you achieve a thick, tempting gravy that tastes just like the traditional recipe.

SERVES 4

1 lb [455 g] grass-fed beef stew meat

1 Tbsp unsweetened 100% cacao powder

1 Tbsp Worcestershire sauce

1 tsp paprika

1 tsp freshly ground black pepper

½ tsp salt

2 sweet onions, such as Vidalia or Maui, diced

10 oz [280 g] assorted mushrooms, such as cremini, shiitake, or hen-of-the-woods, chopped or quartered

½ cup [120 ml] beef broth or Basic Bone Broth (page 59)

½ cup [120 g] sour cream

½ cup [20 g] chopped flat-leaf parsley

Place the beef in the slow cooker. Add the cacao powder, Worcestershire sauce, paprika, pepper, and salt and toss until the beef is well coated. Layer the onions over the beef, followed by the mushrooms. Pour the broth over the top. Cover the slow cooker and cook on the high setting for 3½ to 4 hours, until the beef and mushrooms are very tender and the beef is fork-tender.

Transfer the stroganoff to a large serving bowl and stir in the sour cream, or divide the stew among four bowls and top each serving with 2 tablespoons sour cream. Garnish with the parsley and serve immediately.

Nutritional Stats per Serving

316 calories, 28 g protein, 21 g carbohydrates, 14 g fat (4 g saturated fat), 62 mg cholesterol, 8 g sugars, 6 g fiber, 340 mg sodium

CASHEW NUT MOLE WITH CHICKEN AND SWEET POTATOES

In Mexico, *mole* is just another word for sauce, and there are many varieties from red to green to chocolate (my favorite!). Oaxacan mole (or chocolate mole) is slowly cooked over several days and gets its rich dark color not only from chocolate, but also from a wide variety of dried chiles, sesame seeds, nuts, and fruits. This faster, simplified version is ideal for the slow cooker and can even be used as a stand-alone sauce for dipping raw vegetables. Preparing savory meals with unsweetened chocolate is a smarter way to get more chocolate into your diet. You'll benefit from the cacao flavanols that improve cognitive function, specifically memory. Other compounds in chocolate (like theobromine and caffeine) improve mood. With recipes like this one, you can still enjoy chocolate without the processed white sugar that is linked to depression and chronic illness.

SERVES 8

4 sweet potatoes, about 2½ lb [1.2 kg], peeled and diced

½ cup [120 ml] chicken broth or vegetable broth

½ cup [130 g] cashew butter or peanut butter

½ cup [70 g] raisins

¼ cup [35 g] sesame seeds

2 Tbsp chopped chipotle chiles in adobo

4 garlic cloves, halved

Juice of 2 oranges

2 Tbsp apple cider vinegar

1 tsp salt

1 lb [455 g] boneless, skinless chicken breasts, cubed

2 red or green bell peppers, seeded, deribbed, and chopped

2 oz [55 g] dark 70% chocolate

Put the sweet potatoes in the slow cooker. Put the broth, cashew butter, raisins, sesame seeds, chipotle, garlic, orange juice, vinegar, and salt in a blender or food processor and process until smooth. Pour over the sweet potatoes in the slow cooker. Cover the slow cooker and cook on the low setting for 2 to 2½ hours, until the sauce thickens and the sweet potatoes are tender.

Add the chicken and bell peppers and toss until well coated. Cook on the low setting for 2 to 2½ hours more, until the chicken is cooked through. During the last 10 minutes of cooking, stir in the chocolate. Stir again once or twice before serving.

Spoon into bowls and serve immediately.

Nutritional Stats per Serving
301 calories, 18 g protein, 27 g carbohydrates, 15 g fat (4 g saturated fat), 37 mg cholesterol, 12 g sugars, 4 g fiber, 391 mg sodium

SUSTAIN AND PROTECT

MEET THE INGREDIENTS:
Ginger, Garlic, Cabbage, Eggs, Seeds

CHAPTER 5

SUSTAIN AND PROTECT

Improve Organ Function and Fortify Immunity

Want to stay in flow state? Sustaining and protecting the status quo is easy when you eat right. Eating well at home, maintaining your exercise routine, and sleeping deeply can keep your life in the sweet spot, and including sustaining foods, like the ones you'll see in this chapter, will do just that. A bounty of diverse whole foods that deliver high levels of various antioxidants should always be a part of the healing eating equation. But you'll also want to add more adaptogenic foods, like ginger, to help keep you in the zone and even take your immunity to the next level. Maintain balance with sustaining proteins like amino-rich eggs that protect on many levels, from organs to brain function, and with detoxing vegetables like cabbages that gently cleanse with sulfur compounds.

Ginger, Garlic, Cabbage, Eggs, Seeds

Ginger
Improve and Fortify

Zesty ginger can easily perk up plain proteins and vegetables, but this healthy "catch-all" root also has amazing healing potential. A special group of compounds called gingerols, shogaol, and paradols are responsible for its spicy hot flavor and for its health benefits. Ginger is a powerhouse of anti-inflammatory and antioxidative properties with plenty of medicinal research behind it showing that it's beneficial for liver and kidney health, degenerative disorders (arthritis and rheumatism), digestive health (indigestion, constipation, and ulcers), cardiovascular disorders (atherosclerosis and hypertension), and more.

Garlic
Improve and Fortify

Protective delicious garlic contains potent antibacterial, antifungal, and antiparasitic properties—all of which reside in the sulfur compounds that give garlic its pungent taste. Once thought of as a cure-all for cholesterol, garlic is indeed a healing food for blood pressure, but also carries with it a host of added healing benefits including immunity, cardiovascular health, and diabetes prevention. Combine it with onions to boost its effectiveness and add more flavor to all your slow-cooked meals.

Cabbage
Fortify

Like kale, cabbage contains high levels of glucosinolates, sulfur compounds that help to rehab your liver and help keep cholesterol in check at the same time. Look to cabbage as a low-sugar way to ramp up loads of sustaining vitamin C in your diet, with more than 50 percent of your RDA in just 1 cup. Vitamin C helps to build collagen, neurotransmitters, and aid with iron absorption on top of its accepted immunity building qualities. Adults on average still don't get enough vitamin C, even though it's considered a "must have" for the health minded. Apart from C, cabbage also provides high levels of vitamin K, important for bone health and blood clotting.

Eggs
Improve and Fortify

Time to lift the tyranny of the health myth surrounding eggs! An extensive study of 10,000 participants over 10 years shows that egg yolks do not significantly raise blood-serum cholesterol (that's the cholesterol that your body produces vs. the cholesterol already present in foods) as was once thought. This is great news for your health and your cooking, since the rich tasting yolk contains almost all the sustaining nourishment that this *almost* perfect food (it can be an allergen) can deliver. From all eight essential amino acids to choline (wards off depression) to a broad range of B vitamins that people are sorely deficient in—including biotin (a B-complex vitamin important for metabolism), B_{12}, and B_6—eggs have it all, at only around 77 calories each. When shopping for eggs, go for organic, pasture-raised, since cleanliness of chicken pens, their feed, and how they roam are highly regulated.

Seeds
Fortify

Consider seeds as your triple treat when it comes to even energy levels, since they contain high levels of three important macronutrients: fat, fiber, and protein. All three help to anchor blood sugar for steady energy to efficiently power you through your day. Seeds also contain protective micronutrients in high quantities and have been shown in studies to be protective against cardiovascular diseases, diabetes, and metabolic syndrome. Depending on the seed, from hemp to chia, you'll cash in on sustaining minerals like zinc and magnesium, as well as detoxifying fats like omega-3 fatty acids.

SOFT PARMESAN EGG SCRAMBLE

Contrary to old nutritional info, egg yolks are worth their weight in gold. Yolks are a sustaining, protective food because they contain all eight essential amino acids as well as choline, which improves mood, and biotin, which helps to rebalance blood sugar. Best of all, eggs fill you up with their ideal fat-protein combo. If you're tired of plain scrambles, you will delight in this cheesy Parmesan twist that has a fluffy, almost soufflé-like texture. To make it a special brunch option, add a side salad or top with a few slices of smoked salmon.

SERVES 6

10 large eggs

1 cup [240 ml] grass-fed milk or full-fat canned coconut milk

½ cup [15 g] grated Parmesan

¼ tsp salt

¼ tsp freshly ground black pepper

Olive oil cooking spray

Gently whisk together the eggs, milk, Parmesan, salt, and pepper in a large bowl, just enough to break up the egg yolks.

Coat the inside of the slow cooker with the cooking spray. Pour the egg mixture into the slow cooker, cover, and cook on the low setting for 1 hour, until the egg mixture sets around the edges. Uncover the slow cooker and stir gently for 1 to 2 minutes, until soft curds form.

Spoon into bowls and serve immediately.

Nutritional Stats per Serving

182 calories, 15 g protein, 4 g carbohydrates, 10 g fat (4 g saturated fat), 319 mg cholesterol, 4 g sugars, 0 g fiber, 352 mg sodium

BALSAMIC GOJI OATS

Poppy seeds and hempseeds add texture and healthy fats to this unusual but delicious take on your morning oats. Poppy seeds aren't just for the tops of bagels and desserts; they are an unsung fountain of nutrition. They contain high levels of grounding nutrients (even in small amounts) like calcium, iron, protein, and fiber. Hempseeds, like poppy seeds, also contain these same nutrients, plus the addition of zinc and magnesium.

SERVES 4

1 cup [160 g] steel-cut oats

¼ cup [60 ml] balsamic vinegar

2 Tbsp brown sugar or stevia

2 Tbsp poppy seeds or hempseeds

½ cup [60 g] goji berries or ¼ cup [35 g] dried cherries

Place the oats and 4 cups [960 ml] water in the slow cooker, cover, and cook on the high setting for 2 to 2½ hours, until the oats are tender. Stir in the balsamic vinegar, brown sugar, poppy seeds, and goji berries. Spoon into bowls and serve immediately.

Nutritional Stats per Serving
303 calories, 11 g protein, 46 g carbohydrates, 7 g fat (0 g saturated fat), 0 mg cholesterol, 14 g sugars, 10 g fiber, 45 mg sodium

PROSCIUTTO EGGS WITH KALE

Savory prosciutto turns sunny-side up eggs into something special. In both the French and Italian culinary traditions, salty pork is the ideal flavor pairing with bitter kale and other cruciferous vegetables, making this dish an appropriate, more veggie-centric replacement for your standard bacon and eggs. Eggs are a very sustaining food since they have good amounts of fat (for brain health) and protein (which is muscle building), two macro-nutrients that help you to feel fuller longer; plus, of course, they have every single B vitamin.

SERVES 4

4 cups [60 g] coarsely chopped kale

1½ cups [360 ml] marinara sauce

2 slices prosciutto, chopped

4 large eggs

Put the kale in the slow cooker. Spoon the marinara sauce over the top, then scatter in the prosciutto. Crack the eggs and carefully place them over the marinara sauce mixture, spacing them evenly apart. Cover the slow cooker and cook on the high setting for 1 to 1½ hours, until the kale softens and the egg whites are cooked through but the yolks are still soft. Serve immediately.

Nutritional Stats per Serving
222 calories, 13 g protein, 13 g carbohydrates, 8 g fat (2 g saturated fat), 194 mg cholesterol, 4 g sugars, 1 g fiber, 591 mg sodium

GINGER-SPIKED SPAGHETTI SQUASH WITH PECANS

Pasta is low in nutrition, but tastes oh so good. Spaghetti squash is a great mimic for pasta lovers to get their fix without all the carbs. Just cook it up and shred it with a fork to get fine threads that are just like angel-hair pasta. Spaghetti squash can be bland, but here it gets a flavor spike from ginger, a mega anti-inflammatory root. Ginger also happens to be an adaptogen (see page 13), so it can calm inflammation and soothe stomach problems, heartburn, and motion sickness. Leftovers can double as a veggie-rich breakfast served hot or cold.

SERVES 8

2 Tbsp brown sugar

2 Tbsp grated fresh ginger

1 tsp ground cinnamon

½ tsp salt

¼ tsp freshly ground black pepper

1 spaghetti squash, about 3 lb [1.4 kg], halved lengthwise and seeded

2 Tbsp grass-fed butter, cut into slices

1 cup [120 g] chopped pecans

Pour ½ cup [120 ml] water into the slow cooker. Stir together the brown sugar, ginger, cinnamon, salt, and pepper in a small bowl. Sprinkle the sugar mixture over the cut sides of the squash halves, then dot with the butter.

Place the spaghetti squash halves skin-side down in the slow cooker (you may need to stack them). Cover the slow cooker and cook on the high setting for 4 to 4½ hours, until the squash is tender. Transfer the squash to a cutting board and let cool for 10 minutes. Shred the squash with two forks, then return to the slow cooker and toss with any residual cooking liquid.

Transfer to a serving platter and sprinkle with the pecans. Serve immediately.

Nutritional Stats per Serving
182 calories, 2 g protein, 11 g carbohydrates, 16 g fat (5 g saturated fat), 0 mg cholesterol, 5 g sugars, 3 g fiber, 161 mg sodium

POPPY SEED CITRUS SALMON OVER BEETS

Now that you're opting for simple, healthy slow-cooked meals, here's a way to make the prep easier too! An inexpensive Japanese mandoline—that's also dishwasher-friendly—will make your slicing and dicing a piece of cake. It easily cut root vegetables, like beets, into paper-thin slices so they can cook at the same rate as more delicate proteins like fish. Garlic is a healing, stabilizing food since it contains antibacterial compounds that help lower blood pressure, prevent hardening of the arteries, and inhibit the platelet aggregation that can clog blood vessels.

SERVES 4

1 lime

1 lemon

1 grapefruit

2 Tbsp poppy seeds

2 garlic cloves, minced

½ tsp salt

¼ tsp freshly ground black pepper

1½ lb [680 g] beets, peeled and thinly sliced with a mandoline

½ cup [60 ml] vegetable broth or chicken broth

2 Tbsp balsamic vinegar

Four 4-oz [115-g] skin-on salmon fillets

Zest the lime, lemon, and grapefruit and set aside the zests.

Using a chef's knife, cut the peel from the lemon, lime, and grapefruit. To segment the citrus, work over a large bowl. Holding the peeled citrus in your hand, use a small paring knife to slice between the white membranes to free the citrus segments and allow them to drop into the bowl as you continue onto the next segment. Repeat with the remaining citrus. Set aside.

In a small bowl, stir together the poppy seeds, garlic, citrus zests, salt, and pepper. Set aside.

Put the beets, broth, and vinegar in the slow cooker and toss well. Spread the beets out in an even layer. Place the salmon fillets skin-side down on top of the beets. Spoon the citrus-zest mixture evenly over the salmon. Cover the slow cooker and cook on the low setting for 2 to 2½ hours, until the salmon flakes when pressed with a fork and the beets are tender.

Transfer the salmon to plates and top with the citrus segments. Serve immediately with the beets.

Nutritional Stats per Serving

286 calories, 26 g protein, 23 g carbohydrates, 9 g fat (1 g saturated fat), 62 mg cholesterol, 16 g sugars, 6 g fiber, 503 mg sodium

SPICY BUTTERED SALMON WITH SNOW PEAS

Hot wing fans will love this spicy salmon, which uses the same tangy hot sauce, Frank's, found in the popular bar food. If you're more of a spicy tuna roll fan, use Sriracha instead and swap the butter for an olive oil–based mayo. Cabbage, part of the cruciferous family, is delicious raw but better for you when cooked. Cooking cabbage increases its ability to bind with bile acids, which helps to regulate blood cholesterol levels.

SERVES 8

2 Tbsp grass-fed butter, at room temperature

2 Tbsp hot sauce, such as Frank's RedHot or Sriracha

1 lb [455 g] snow peas, trimmed

2 cups [120 g] thinly sliced cabbage

1 Tbsp olive oil

2 garlic cloves, minced

One 1-in [2.5-cm] piece fresh ginger, minced

¼ tsp freshly ground black pepper

Eight 4-oz [115-g] skin-on salmon fillets

In a small bowl, mash together the butter and the hot sauce with the back of a small spoon. Set aside.

Put the snow peas, cabbage, olive oil, garlic, ginger, and black pepper in the slow cooker and toss well. Place the salmon fillets skin-side down on top of the snow-pea mixture. Spread the spiced butter over the top of the salmon fillets. Cover the slow cooker and cook on the low setting for 1½ to 2 hours, until the salmon flakes when pressed with a fork.

Transfer the fillets to plates and serve immediately with the snow peas.

Nutritional Stats per Serving

235 calories, 24 g protein, 6 g carbohydrates, 12 g fat (3 g saturated fat), 62 mg cholesterol, 4 g sugars, 2 g fiber, 131 mg sodium

CRAB CAKES WITH GINGER MAYO

Proteins that also contain the right kinds of fat, like omega-3s, can do double duty. They protect lean muscle mass and also add anti-inflammatory fats that are essential for healthy glowing skin and collagen production. Cooking with canned crab is a simple way to boost omega-3 fatty-acid intake, since it comes already cooked when you purchase it. Homemade mayo, made with a nutrient-rich egg, makes a superior dipping sauce since it also contains healthy, sustaining fats that ground your hunger.

SERVES 6

2 eggs

1 cup [240 ml] safflower or light olive oil

One 1-in [2.5-cm] piece fresh ginger, peeled and minced

½ tsp low-sodium seasoning salt

½ cup [6 g] chopped fresh flat-leaf parsley

2 Tbsp chia seeds

1 lb [455 g] pasteurized cooked crabmeat

½ cup [55 g] gluten-free bread crumbs

To make the mayonnaise, put 1 egg, the oil, ginger, and ¼ tsp of the seasoning salt in a tall jar. Using an immersion blender, place the blender head into the jar and rest it on the inside bottom of the jar as you blend. Blend for 30 seconds, without lifting up the blender head, until a thick white cloud forms and all the oil is incorporated. Set aside.

Put the parsley, the remaining egg, ¼ cup [60 g] of the homemade mayonnaise, the chia seeds, and the remaining ¼ tsp seasoning salt in a large bowl and stir together with a wooden spoon. Add the crabmeat and half of the bread crumbs, gently tossing until evenly mixed. Form the crab mixture into 6 patties. Spread the remaining bread crumbs in a shallow bowl and press the patties into them to coat both sides.

Place the crab cakes in the slow cooker, cover, and cook on the low setting for 1 to 1½ hours, until the cakes are warm.

Transfer the crab cakes to a plate and serve immediately with the remaining mayonnaise.

Nutritional Stats per Serving
249 calories, 13 g protein, 8 g carbohydrates, 18 g fat (2 g saturated fat), 109 mg cholesterol, 0 g sugars, 0 g fiber, 509 mg sodium

GINGER SESAME CHICKEN WITH ASIAN COLESLAW

Ginger, a top anti-inflammatory root, is the perfect way to perk up bland chicken. Historically, ginger has been a folk remedy for seasickness and motion sickness. According to medical studies, it's no wonder, since it contains gingerol, a compound that actually calms spasms that can leave your stomach in knots. Sesame seeds, like other seeds, can help sustain us, since they are high in iron (key in transporting oxygen to tissues), which keeps us feeling and looking vibrant.

SERVES 4

1 lb [455 kg] bone-in, skinless chicken thighs

3 Tbsp grated fresh ginger

2 Tbsp honey

2 Tbsp reduced-sodium tamari

¼ cup sesame seeds

2 jalapeño chiles, seeded and minced

2 garlic cloves, minced

8 oz [230 g] coleslaw mix

3 Tbsp olive oil–based mayonnaise

1 Tbsp Asian sesame oil

1 Tbsp apple cider vinegar

Put the chicken thighs in the slow cooker. In a small bowl, stir together the ginger, honey, tamari, sesame seeds, half of the jalapeños, and the garlic. Cover the slow cooker and cook on the low setting for 1½ to 2 hours, until the chicken is cooked through and no longer pink in the center.

While the chicken is cooking, prepare the coleslaw. In a large bowl, toss together the slaw mix, mayonnaise, sesame oil, vinegar, and remaining jalapeños.

Transfer the chicken to a platter and serve immediately with the coleslaw.

Nutritional Stats per Serving
333 calories, 27 g protein, 15 g carbohydrates, 18 g fat (3 g saturated fat), 84 mg cholesterol, 10 g sugars, 2 g fiber, 535 mg sodium

CRANBERRY ORANGE CHICKEN WITH CABBAGE

The humble cabbage, which makes up the base for this dish, is chock-full of healing nutrients, including vitamins A, B6, B1, B2, manganese, fiber, potassium, and folate. Tart frozen cranberries, paired with anti-inflammatory superstar ginger, add a flavor blast to this chicken dish. Whole cranberries are nothing like the overly sweet dried version that is almost like candy in disguise. Unsweetened cranberries were traditionally used by American Indians to treat bladder and kidney disease, which current medical research now shows is due to the pigments that reside in their ruby red skins. You'll love their tanginess here.

SERVES 8

8 oz [230 g] shredded red cabbage, thinly sliced

Four 6-oz [170-g] boneless, skinless chicken breasts

2 cups [220 g] frozen cranberries

Zest and juice of 4 oranges

¼ cup [85 g] honey

One 1-in [2.5-cm] piece fresh ginger, peeled and minced

2 tsp fresh thyme leaves or 1 tsp dried thyme

½ tsp salt

¼ tsp freshly ground black pepper

Put the cabbage in the slow cooker and place the chicken breasts on top. In a large bowl, stir together the cranberries, orange zest and juice, honey, ginger, thyme, salt, and pepper. Spoon the cranberry mixture over the top of the chicken. Cover the slow cooker and cook on the low setting for 4 to 4½ hours, until the chicken is cooked through and no longer pink in the center.

Transfer the chicken to plates and serve immediately with the cabbage and sauce on the side.

Nutritional Stats per Serving

345 calories, 37 g protein, 38 g carbohydrates, 4 g fat (1 g saturated fat), 108 mg cholesterol, 29 g sugars, 5 g fiber, 506 mg sodium

STUFFED GINGERED CABBAGE ROLLS

For healthy glowing skin, consider cruciferous vegetables like cabbage your new best friend, even when you're not on a cleanse. This comfort-food meal can also double as a weight-balancing dish, since it's surprisingly low-calorie yet filling at the same time. Cruciferous vegetables, like the cabbage in this recipe, are a must-have ingredient for anyone who wants a wide range of nutritional benefits, including vitamins from A to D and plenty more.

SERVES 6

½ cup [50 g] old-fashioned rolled oats

1 large egg

¼ tsp garlic salt

¼ tsp freshly ground black pepper

One 3-lb [1.4-kg] head napa cabbage

One 28-oz [794-g] can diced tomatoes

1 cup [240 ml] Basic Bone Broth (page 59)

2 Tbsp tomato paste

1 lb [455 g] grass-fed ground beef or buffalo

4 carrots, peeled, grated

2 stalks celery, chopped

4 scallions, chopped, white and green parts

½ cup [6 g] packed fresh flat-leaf parsley leaves or cilantro leaves

2 Tbsp minced fresh ginger

Stir together the oats, egg, garlic salt, and pepper in a large bowl. Let rest for 30 minutes to allow the oats to soften.

Meanwhile, prepare the remaining ingredients. Bring a large stockpot filled halfway with water to a boil. Trim the tough root end of the cabbage so that you can easily remove 24 of the outer leaves (reserve the remaining cabbage for another use). When the water boils, turn off the heat and add half of the leaves, pressing to submerge them in the hot water. Cover the stockpot and let soak for 4 to 5 minutes, until the leaves begin to soften. Remove the cabbage leaves with tongs and drain them in a colander. Bring the water to a boil again and parcook the remaining cabbage leaves. Drain them in a colander. Repeat with remaining leaves. (Alternatively, working in batches, wrap the leaves in a damp paper towel and microwave for 1 minute, until softened.) Set aside to cool.

Put the diced tomatoes, broth, and tomato paste in the slow cooker and mix together.

Add the beef, carrots, celery, scallions, parsley, and ginger to the bowl with the oats and mix together with your fingers. Place a cabbage leaf on a cutting board and trim off the tough bottom. Place 3 Tbsp of the meat mixture close to the bottom edge of the leaf and roll up. Tuck in the edges and place the cabbage roll seam-side down over the tomato mixture in the slow cooker. Repeat with the remaining leaves and filling.

Cover the slow cooker and cook on the low setting for 3 to 3½ hours, until the filling is cooked through and no longer pink in the middle. To check for doneness, slice the cabbage roll open with a paring knife.

Transfer the stuffed cabbage to soup plates and serve immediately.

Nutritional Stats per Serving
305 calories, 23 g protein, 26 g carbohydrates, 13 g fat (1 g saturated fat), 74 mg cholesterol, 12 g sugars, 7 g fiber, 256 mg sodium

FALL HARVEST POT ROAST

Pot roast is a heartwarming slow cooker classic! But even this traditional recipe can benefit from a few tweaks, such as swapping grass-fed beef for conventional beef. If sky-high grocery bills are getting you down, consider sharing a large online order of grass-fed beef with a friend or two. It is less expensive to order directly from farms, and many of them offer deals that include pasture-raised pork and chicken.

SERVES 10

One 5-lb [2.3-kg] grass-fed beef rump roast

1 tsp garlic salt

1 tsp paprika

½ tsp freshly ground black pepper

¼ cup [70 g] tomato paste

¼ cup [60 ml] white or red wine

¼ cup [60 ml] Basic Bone Broth (page 59) or beef broth

1 lb [455 g] parsnips, peeled and chopped

2 onions, chopped

Cloves from 1 head garlic, peeled

Put the roast on a plate and sprinkle with the garlic salt, paprika, and pepper. Using a spatula, spread the tomato paste all over the roast. Place the roast in the slow cooker and pour the wine and broth around the roast. Scatter the parsnips, onions, and garlic cloves around the roast. Cover the slow cooker and cook on the low setting for 6 to 8 hours, until the roast is very tender and the sauce has thickend around the roast.

Remove the roast from the slow cooker and slice against the grain into thick slices. Transfer to a platter. Spoon over the sauce and vegetables remaining in the slow cooker and serve.

Nutritional Stats per Serving

377 calories, 45 g protein, 13 g carbohydrates, 13 g fat (5 g saturated fat), 120 mg cholesterol, 4 g sugars, 3 g fiber, 439 mg sodium

ALL SYSTEMS GO AND GLOW

MEET THE INGREDIENTS:
Hot Chiles, Turmeric, Avocado, Fats, Lavender

ALL SYSTEMS GO AND GLOW

Revitalize and Protect Skin, Eyes, and Hair

Glowing skin and eyes along with shining hair are the calling cards of health. Eating for beauty may seem only skin deep, but the foods that benefit your outside help your insides as well. Beauty foods that provide high levels of vitamin A, C, and E, along with fats like omega-3s and compounds like curcumin, are heavily featured here, and they have multiple functions, as you've learned along the way. Eating for beauty and general health are one and the same, but keep in mind that certain nutrients play a key role in the look and feel of skin and hair.

These include anti-inflammatory fats like omega-3s, Vitamin C, and copper, which is skin-protective against sun and wind, and also increases the bioavailability of selenium—the superstar mineral for hair and thyroid health. Vitamin A, synthesized from carotenoids, is protective against sun damage, particularly UV rays. Curcumin, the active ingredient in turmeric, has been used topically for centuries in India to cure psoriasis and deal with acne. It's even used today for an over-the-counter psoriasis cream because of its ability to squelch inflammation.

Hot Chiles, Turmeric, Avocado, Fats, Lavender

Hot Chiles

Revitalize

Hot chiles get their fiery heat from the active compound capsaicin, an alkaloid compound that burns on contact and is used not only to turn up the heat in hot wings and barbecue sauces, but also as a warming agent in topical arthritis creams. Hot chiles, especially red, orange, and yellow, are also high in vitamin C, the super skin nutrient that can protect your skin against sun and wind damage. If you're looking to tame an overactive appetite, spicy chiles can work as a natural appetite suppressant, and they happen to be incredibly low in calories at just 26 calories per cup.

Turmeric

Revitalize and Protect

Think of turmeric as the "everything" spice, a supermodel of healing foods, the top adaptogen that will never go out of fashion in health circles. It has a whopping 700 medical studies showing a long list of benefits, covering everything from cancer to obesity, diabetes, and skin ailments. It's included in this chapter since it's a wonder for healthy skin, but also liberally sprinkled throughout the book because its detoxifying power fits into every chapter and can be sprinkled into many recipes. Turmeric's active ingredient, curcumin, continues to awe medical science; the only concern is its bioavailability. Combining it with pepper (as mentioned earlier) along with a fat source certainly increases uptake, but studies show that even with low absorption it's still a wunderkind of healing.

Avocado

Protect

Avocados, a delectable fatty fruit, have a unique mix of health-promoting qualities. A blend of MUFA fats, loads of fiber, and plenty of antioxidants like lutein and zeaxanthin explains why avocados have been known to ward off metabolic syndrome, a combination of medical conditions including obesity, high blood pressure, high blood sugar, and high cholesterol. Avocados are a top skin-healing food because they are high in vitamin E—a fat-soluble nutrient that works synergistically with vitamin C to protect your skin from free-radical damage while it moisturizes from the inside out. So combining avocado with kale, citrus, red bell pepper, and other vitamin C-rich foods is a boon for your skin *and* your dinner table.

Fats

Protect

Fearing fat is a thing of the past, now that we know how important good-quality fats are for us in many ways, including grounding hunger, helping absorb nutrients, and improving and protecting skin quality. Older nutritional science only gives a thumbs-up to certain unsaturated fats like safflower, olive, and sesame oils, but through more recent research on grass-fed meats and dairy, you can welcome beef and butter back into your life, if you go grass-fed. Grass-fed butter has a very different molecular makeup compared to its corn-fed counterpart. Grass-fed dairy (and beef for that matter) is high in omega-3s and CLA (conjugated linoleic acid) that may reduce body-fat levels.

Lavender

Revitalize and Protect

Lavender has been used for centuries as a healing herb for topical skin use and continues to be at the top of the list when it comes to aromatherapy. In culinary circles, lavender is prized for its pungent yet floral scent that also carries with it a hint of rosemary (both come from the same family, mint). Lavender is high in antibacterial qualities and thus lends soothing to the nervous system.

SUNNY-SIDE UP EGGS WITH SWEET POTATO FRIES

This updated version of fried eggs and hash browns swaps in vitamin A–rich sweet potato fries for hash browns and tops it all off with eggs, which are rich in healing fats and a wide range of antioxidants for your skin, like biotin, a B vitamin that helps to nourish, skin, nails, and hair. The addition of kale not only gets a serving of greens into your morning, but also adds a super array of nutrients that are body beautiful like vitamin A, which can protect skin and help with overall detox when used by the liver.

SERVES 4

Olive oil cooking spray

4 cups [60 g] chopped kale, such as curly or lacinato

One 20-oz [566-g] bag frozen sweet potato fries

4 large eggs

½ cup [150 g] kimchi or ½ cup [33 g] jarred spicy tomato salsa

Coat the inside of the slow cooker with the cooking spray. Put the kale in the slow cooker, spreading it into an even layer, and top with the sweet potato fries. Cover the slow cooker and cook on the high setting for 1 to 1½ hours, until the fries are hot and the kale is wilted. Crack the eggs and carefully place them over the sweet potatoes, spacing them evenly apart. Cover the slow cooker and cook on the high setting for 30 minutes more, until the egg whites are cooked through but the yolks are still soft.

Using a spatula, transfer the eggs to plates along with the fries and kale. Pile a big pinch of the kimchi alongside each and serve immediately.

Nutritional Stats per Serving
250 calories, 9 g protein, 32 g carbohydrates, 10 g fat (1 g saturated fat), 186 mg cholesterol, 7 g sugars, 4 g fiber, 451 mg sodium

BLUEBERRY BUTTERMILK AMARANTH

Amaranth, a tasty grain from South America that reminds me of corn, makes an excellent creamy porridge. And it will help you get your glow on with its beautifying nutrients like selenium, which aids with hair growth; manganese that boosts your thyroid (and which can play a part in healthy skin and mood); and plenty of fiber that is helpful for weight maintenance and general detox. Floral, antibacterial, calming lavender pairs beautifully with juicy blueberries, which contain plant nutrients that are also protective for your eyes, as they guard the retina from oxygen damage.

SERVES 8

1 cup [180 g] amaranth

2 Tbsp grass-fed butter or coconut oil

1 Tbsp honey or 2 tsp stevia

4 cups [560 g] fresh blueberries

1 cup [240 ml] buttermilk

4 Brazil nuts, chopped

1 tsp culinary lavender

Put the amaranth, 4 cups [960 ml] water, butter, and honey in the slow cooker and mix together. Cover the slow cooker and cook on the high setting for 2 to 2½ hours, until the grains are tender.

Spoon into bowls and divide the blueberries among the bowls. Drizzle each serving with 2 Tbsp buttermilk and sprinkle with the Brazil nuts and lavender. Serve immediately.

Nutritional Stats per Serving
403 calories, 11 g protein, 57 g carbohydrates, 16 g fat (6 g saturated fat), 20 mg cholesterol, 18 g sugars, 7 g fiber, 64 mg sodium

TOMATO ORANGE SOUP WITH LAVENDER

Standard canned tomato soup has zero imagination, high levels of sodium, and lacks the freshness of this more unique orange-spiked tomato soup. Tomato, a healing lycopene-rich fruit that's good for your skin, pairs wonderfully with oranges, which are rich in vitamin C and also skin-protective. If you have an abundance of fresh tomatoes, you can use those as well; about six beefsteaks are the equivalent of two big cans. Lavender is an "it" ingredient that you'll find in many beauty products because of its potent antibacterial and antifungal agents. Its unique clean smell (prized in aromatherapy) calms to ease the stress and anxiety that can cause wrinkles while adding a floral note to this soup.

SERVES 6

One 28-oz [794-g] can diced tomatoes

4 cups [960 ml] Basic Bone Broth (page 59) or vegetable broth

2 oranges, peeled and chopped

2 Tbsp tomato paste

3 Tbsp extra-virgin olive oil

4 garlic cloves, minced

1 tsp culinary lavender

Rice crackers or corn chips for serving

Put the diced tomatoes, broth, oranges, tomato paste, oil, garlic, and lavender in the slow cooker and stir well. Cover the slow cooker and cook on the low setting for 2 to 2½ hours, until the oranges start to break down. Using an immersion blender, purée until smooth.

Spoon into bowls and serve immediately with rice crackers or corn chips.

CHEF'S NOTE: To make this a more filling meal, add 4 oz [115 g] peeled, deveined medium shrimp.

Nutritional Stats per Serving
246 calories, 11 g protein, 19 g carbohydrates, 10 g fat (4 g saturated fat), 0 mg cholesterol, 12 g sugars, 4 g fiber, 253 mg sodium

ARTISANAL CHEDDAR CHEESE SOUP

Oil-rich cheese and grass-fed milk paired with vitamin A–rich sweet potato makes the base for this tangy soup, with skin health in mind since both fats and vitamin A are very skin-protective. The sweet potato and cornstarch (organic to avoid GMOs) combo makes the soup smooth and creamy so that the amount of calorie-dense cheese stays in check. Turmeric, a superfood for skin used in psoriasis creams and even as a natural acne treatment, enriches the golden color of this soup. Using hot chiles as a garnish adds a little fat-burning power.

SERVES 8

2 cups [480 ml] grass-fed milk

2 cups [480 ml] Basic Bone Broth (page 59), or low-sodium chicken or vegetable broth

2 Tbsp organic cornstarch or organic potato starch

1 Tbsp Worcestershire sauce

1 Tbsp hot sauce (optional)

½ tsp ground turmeric

½ tsp freshly ground black pepper

½ tsp dried mustard

¾ tsp garlic salt

2 large sweet potatoes, about 1¼ lb [570 g], peeled and grated

8 oz [230 g] artisanal cheddar cheese, preferably grass-fed, shredded

1 red bell pepper, seeded, deribbed, and diced

2 jalapeño chiles, seeded and minced

Put the milk, broth, cornstarch, Worcestershire sauce, hot sauce (if using), turmeric, pepper, mustard, and garlic salt in the slow cooker and mix together. Add the sweet potatoes. Cover the slow cooker and cook on the low setting for 2 to 2½ hours, until the mixture is hot and the sweet potato is tender. Stir in the cheese until melted. Using an immersion blender, purée until smooth.

Spoon into bowls. Sprinkle with the red bell peppers and jalapeños and serve immediately.

Nutritional Stats per Serving
295 calories, 16 g protein, 13 g carbohydrates, 17 g fat (11 g saturated fat), 50 mg cholesterol, 6 g sugars, 2 g fiber, 452 mg sodium

CHIPOTLE PUMPKIN CHILI

Pumpkin purée is a healthy and clever way to add thickness to soups without adding flour. Pumpkin is also a smart food for skin health, since it's rich in disease-preventing beta-carotene—a super skin nutrient since it gets turned into vitamin A (retinol) in your body. Spicy chiles like chipotle get their heat from the healing ingredient capsaicin, which shrinks tumor cells in medical trials and works as a major anti-inflammatory for all your organs.

SERVES 6

4 scallions, chopped, green and white parts

1 Tbsp coconut or olive oil, or grass-fed butter

2 garlic cloves, minced

½ tsp ground turmeric

½ tsp freshly ground black pepper

One 15-oz [425-g] can 100% pure pumpkin purée

One 15-oz [425-g] can chickpeas, drained and rinsed

4 cups [960 ml] chicken broth or vegetable broth

1 Tbsp tomato paste

1 Tbsp chopped chipotle chiles in adobo

1 Tbsp mild chili powder

1 cup [85 g] small gluten-free pasta, such as shells or stars

2 avocados, peeled, pitted, and diced

Put the scallions, oil, garlic, turmeric, and pepper in the slow cooker and mix together. Cover the slow cooker and cook on the high setting for 30 minutes to allow the scallions to release their flavor. Stir in the pumpkin purée, chickpeas, broth, tomato paste, chipotles, chili powder, and pasta. Cook on the low setting for 2 to 2½ hours more, stirring once or twice, until the broth thickens and the pasta is tender.

Spoon into bowls and scatter the avocados over the top. Serve immediately.

Nutritional Stats per Serving

325 calories, 13 g protein, 45 g carbohydrates, 12 g fat (4 g saturated fat), 3 mg cholesterol, 7 g sugars, 13 g fiber, 172 mg sodium

CAULIFLOWER SRIRACHA RICE WITH BLUE CHEESE CRUMBLES

Mellow cauliflower rice gets the hot wing treatment with tangy, spicy Sriracha and rich blue cheese crumbles. Sriracha, a Thai sauce made with plenty of hot chiles and vinegar, contains the active compound capsaicin, which produces a hot sensation and gives it its body-beautiful properties—it helps with sinus pain, fights general inflammation, and provides high levels of vitamin C for skin health and natural appetite control for weight loss and increased calorie burn. Sriracha can be located in Asian specialty stores or in the international aisle of your local grocery store.

SERVES 8

1 large head cauliflower, about 2½ lb [1.2 kg], cut into florets

½ cup [120 ml] Basic Bone Broth (page 59), beef broth, or chicken broth

3 to 4 Tbsp Sriracha sauce

2 Tbsp grass-fed butter or coconut oil

½ tsp garlic salt

1 cup [120 g] crumbled blue cheese

Working in batches, put the cauliflower florets in a food processor and pulse until the pieces resemble the size of rice kernels. Transfer the cauliflower to the slow cooker. Stir in the broth, Sriracha, butter, and garlic salt. Cover the slow cooker and cook on the high setting for 2 to 2½ hours, until the cauliflower is tender. Sprinkle with the blue cheese, cover the slow cooker, and let rest for 5 minutes, until the cheese melts.

Transfer to a large platter and serve immediately.

Nutritional Stats per Serving

127 calories, 6 g protein, 6 g carbohydrates, 8 g fat (5 g saturated fat), 20 mg cholesterol, 3 g sugars, 2 g fiber, 447 mg sodium

CREAMY ASPARAGUS ARTICHOKE DIP

This dish is inspired by one of my favorite party foods: creamy spinach dip. Making it with bone broth gives it serious savoriness, and the olive oil–based mayo is rich in skin-healing MUFAs (that's monounsaturated fatty acids), which will also satisfy your hunger. Fresh jalapeños add zing and the nutrient vitamin C, perfect for giving skin that healthy glow. Like all spicy chiles, jalapeños are rich in the healing compound capsaicin, which may help to repair liver damage—good news for clearer skin, since the liver is the number 2 detox organ responsible for removing toxins that play havoc with skin health.

SERVES 6

One 9-oz [255-g] package frozen artichoke hearts, defrosted and chopped

1 bunch asparagus, trimmed and finely chopped

4 jalapeños, seeded and minced

½ cup [120 ml] Basic Bone Broth (page 59) or chicken broth

1 tsp paprika

¼ tsp salt

¼ tsp freshly ground black pepper

1 cup [240 g] olive oil–based mayonnaise or homemade mayo (page 136, omit the ginger)

½ cup [120 ml] Greek yogurt

½ cup [20 g] chopped fresh basil

½ cup [30 g] grated pecorino cheese

Crackers or corn chips for serving

Put the artichokes, asparagus, jalapeños, broth, paprika, salt, and pepper in the slow cooker and mix together. Cover the slow cooker and cook on the high heat setting for 1 to 1½ hours, until the asparagus is tender. Stir in the mayonnaise, yogurt, basil, and pecorino cheese. Cover the slow cooker and cook on the low setting for 2 hours, until the edges of the dip start to brown.

Serve immediately in the slow cooker with crackers or chips.

Nutritional Stats per Serving

244 calories, 5 g protein, 21 g carbohydrates, 21 g fat (3 g saturated fat), 15 mg cholesterol, 2 g sugars, 5 g fiber, 359 mg sodium

HOT SHRIMP COCKTAIL
WITH HORSERADISH

Shrimp cocktail is a traditional seafood appetizer, but when prepped in
your healing slow cooker, it becomes a tantalizing meal using all the same
flavors. Horseradish, traditionally used in cocktail sauce, is a superfood
for the immune system. The spicy root contains glucosinolates, the same
healing sulfur compound that you find in kale, along with powerful antimicrobial compounds.

SERVES 8

2 lb [910 g] peeled, deveined medium shrimp

1 cup [240 ml] cocktail sauce

4 cups [80 g] baby spinach, chopped

1 red bell pepper, seeded, deribbed, and diced

1 Tbsp grated horseradish

½ tsp ground turmeric

¼ tsp freshly ground black pepper

24 romaine lettuce leaves, about 1 lb [455 g]

½ cup [65 g] hempseeds

Place the shrimp, cocktail sauce, spinach, bell pepper, horseradish,
turmeric, and pepper in the slow cooker and toss well. Cover the slow
cooker and cook on the low setting for 2 to 2½ hours, until the shrimp
are cooked through.

Place the lettuce leaves on a platter. Divide the shrimp and sauce among
the lettuce and top with the hempseeds.

Nutritional Stats per Serving
237 calories, 25 g protein, 17 g carbohydrates, 6 g fat (0 g saturated fat),
143 mg cholesterol, 9 g sugars, 6 g fiber, 490 mg sodium

CHIPOTLE LIME SHREDDED PORK TACOS WITH AVOCADO SALSA

Long-cooked shredded pork is a sumptuous treat. Serve with plenty of toppings that will help your skin shine. Cabbage is high in vitamin C and fatty avocado, with plenty of vitamin E, covers many of the skin-care bases.

SERVES 8

4 cups [240 g] shredded red cabbage, thinly sliced

2 lb [910 g] boneless pork loin, preferably from the butt end

2 Tbsp chopped chipotle chiles in adobo

Zest and juice of 2 limes

4 garlic cloves, minced

½ tsp salt, divided

½ tsp freshly ground black pepper, divided

2 avocados, peeled, pitted, and diced

¼ cup [35 g] minced red onion

2 jalapeño chiles, seeded and minced

24 corn tortillas

Put the cabbage in the slow cooker, spreading it out into an even layer. Place the pork on top of the cabbage and top with the chipotle, half of the lime zest and juice, all the garlic, half the salt, and half the black pepper. Cover the slow cooker and cook on the high setting for 4 to 5½ hours, until the pork is fork-tender. With tongs, transfer the pork to a work surface and let cool.

While the pork is cooking, make the salsa. In a bowl, toss together the avocados, onion, jalapeños, remaining salt, remaining black pepper, and remaining lime zest and juice. Set aside.

Shred the pork with two forks. Return the shredded meat to the slow cooker and toss with the sauce until well coated.

Just before serving, warm the tortillas in a toaster oven or on a gas burner. Divide the pork and cabbage among the tortillas and top with the salsa. Serve immediately.

_____

Nutritional Stats per Serving

410 calories, 26 g protein, 16 g carbohydrates, 16 g fat (4 g saturated fat), 74 mg cholesterol, 2 g sugars, 8 g fiber, 188 mg sodium

TANGY FETA CHICKEN

Chicken is a lean "flavor canvas" that cries out for the sweet hot flavor of peppadew chiles, a pickled pepper from South Africa. Once you pick a jar of peppadews from your local pickle aisle, you'll see what you've been missing. Just wrap this delicious chicken mixture in kale and crunch away. Compounds in peppadews, and all spicy chiles, are not only great for your skin but also heart healthy, since they can help to lower blood pressure.

SERVES 4

1 lb [455 g] boneless, skinless chicken breasts, cut into
1-in [2.5-cm] pieces

1 cup [160 g] pitted black olives, chopped

1 cup [160 g] jarred peppadew chiles or 1 cup [136 g] pickled jalapeño chiles

2 Tbsp grass-fed butter or coconut oil

2 Tbsp apple cider vinegar or balsamic vinegar

1 Tbsp herbes de Provence or Italian seasoning

1 tsp paprika

½ tsp freshly ground black pepper

8 oz [230 g] crumbled feta

1 bunch kale, stemmed

6 scallions, thinly sliced, green and white parts

Put the chicken, olives, peppadews, butter, vinegar, herbes de Provence, paprika, and pepper in the slow cooker and toss well. Cover the slow cooker and cook on the low setting for 1½ to 2 hours, until the chicken is cooked through. Sprinkle with the feta, cover the slow cooker, and let rest for 5 minutes, until the cheese melts.

Arrange the kale leaves on a large platter and divide the chicken mixture between the leaves. Garnish with the scallions and serve immediately.

Nutritional Stats per Serving
330 calories, 34 g protein, 11 g carbohydrates, 17 g fat (10 g saturated fat), 97 mg cholesterol, 2 g sugars, 2 g fiber, 723 mg sodium

STUFFED JALAPEÑOS
WITH CHICKEN SAUSAGE

Jalapeño poppers are a deep-fried treat than can be turned into a healthy meal, as long as you add a hunger-anchoring protein like sausage and lose the deep-fry coating. Jalapeños are high in liquid and vitamin C, and eating them is a great way to get your skin to glow and to add burning power to your evening meal. Set the cooker before you hit the gym, and benefit from the burn inside and out.

SERVES 8

1 grapefruit or 2 oranges

1 lime

8 oz [230 g] cooked chicken sausage or chorizo sausage, chopped

2 cups [40 g] finely chopped kale or spinach

1 large egg

2 garlic cloves, chopped

¼ tsp ground turmeric

1¼ tsp freshly ground black pepper, divided

16 jalapeño chiles, cut in half lengthwise and seeded

2 avocados, peeled, pitted, and diced

Zest the grapefruit or oranges and the lime. To segment the grapefruit, work over a large bowl. Using a chef's knife, cut the peel from the grapefruit. Hold the peeled citrus in your hand. Use a small pairing knife to slice between the white membranes of the grapefruit to free the segments and allow them to drop into the bowl as you continue onto the next segment. Squeeze any excess juice into the bowl with the segments. Squeeze the juice from the lime and add it to the grapefruit, along with all the zest.

In a large bowl, combine the sausage, kale, egg, garlic, turmeric, and 1 tsp pepper and mix well with your hands. Spoon the sausage mixture into the jalapeños shells and place the peppers sausage-side up in the slow cooker. Cover the slow cooker and cook on the low setting for 1 to 1½ hours, until the jalapeños are soft.

CONT'D

While the stuffed jalapeños are cooking, prepare the topping. In a bowl, stir together the avocados, grapefruit mixture, and remaining ¼ tsp black pepper.

Transfer the peppers to a platter, scatter the topping over, and serve immediately.

———————————————————————

Nutritional Stats per Serving
255 calories, 11 g protein, 18 g carbohydrates, 17 g fat (4 g saturated fat), 91 mg cholesterol, 7 g sugars, 6 g fiber, 605 mg sodium

RESOURCES

If you would like to know more about how eating certain foods can change your health for the better, there are many great books and websites I can recommend. Titles with an asterisk (*) are ones in which I've contributed information or recipes.

General Food as Medicine
Bauer, Joy. *Joy Bauer's Food Cures: Eat Right to Get Healthier, Look Younger, and Add Years to Your Life.* * New York: Rodale Books, 2011.

Mateljan, George. *World's Healthiest Foods, 2nd Edition: The Force for Change to Health-Promoting Foods and New Nutrient-Rich Cooking.* New York: GMF Publishing, 2015.

Gut Health and Eating for the Microbiome
Kellman, Raphael. *The Microbiome Diet: The Scientifically Proven Way to Restore Your Gut Health and Achieve Permanent Weight Loss.* New York: DeCapo Lifelong Books, 2015.

Lipski, Elizabeth. *Digestive Wellness: Strengthen the Immune System and Prevent Disease through Healthy Digestion, Fourth Edition.* New York: McGraw-Hill Wellness, 2011.

Lipski, Elizabeth, and Mark Hyman. *Digestion Connection Exclusive Expanded Edition.* New York: Rodale Books, 2013.

Mullin, Gerard E. *The Gut Balance Revolution: Boost Your Metabolism, Restore Your Inner Ecology, and Lose the Weight for Good!* * New York: Rodale Books, 2015.

Pedre, Vincent. *Happy Gut: The Cleansing Program to Help You Lose Weight, Gain Energy, and Eliminate Pain.* New York: William Morrow, 2017.

Herbal Remedies and Adaptogens for Healing

Gladstar, Rosemary. *Rosemary Gladstar's Medicinal Herbs: A Beginner's Guide: 33 Healing Herbs to Know, Grow, and Use.* North Adams, MA: Storey Publishing, 2012.

Pursell, JJ. *The Herbal Apothecary: 100 Medicinal Herbs and How to Use Them.* Portland, OR: Timber Press, 2015.

Winston, David, and Steven Maimes. *Adaptogens: Herbs for Strength, Stamina, and Stress Relief.* Rochester, VT: Healing Arts Press, 2007.

Yance, Donald R. *Adaptogens in Medical Herbalism: Elite Herbs and Natural Compounds for Mastering Stress, Aging, and Chronic Disease.* Rochester, VT: Healing Arts Press, 2013.

Brain Health

Graham, Tyler G., and Drew Ramsey. *The Happiness Diet: A Nutritional Prescription for a Sharp Brain, Balanced Mood, and Lean, Energized Body.** New York: Rodale Books, 2012

Ramsey, Drew. *Eat Complete: The 21 Nutrients That Fuel Brainpower, Boost Weight Loss, and Transform Your Health.** New York: Harper Wave, 2016.

Websites
Dr. Axe: Food Is Medicine
www.draxe.com

Green Med Info: The Science of Natural Healing
www.greenmedinfo.com

Hindawi
www.hindawi.com

Mercola
www.mercola.com

The World's Healthiest Foods
www.whfoods.com

ACKNOWLEDGMENTS

Thank you to my #1 taste tester and supporter, my husband, Uli!
Thank you for seeing me through this wild and crazy food "ride,"
including taking a big chance on my career in the food business,
from restaurant chef to health coach. Thank you to my loving family
and all my supportive friends and neighbors who have cheered me
on during all my book projects, start to finish!

A special thanks to you, "Granny," Patricia Gold, the woman who
raised me with great care, a true grande dame of cooking who not only
taught me how to whip egg whites to perfection, but more importantly,
how to navigate life by working harmoniously with people. I love you!

INDEX